PRAI

WAKE UP, MOM
CAN'T YOU SEE YOUR SON IS AN ADDICT?

"A gripping, heartfelt chronicle of surviving the helplessness and heartache of every parent's worst nightmare. A must-read for anyone with a child struggling with addiction."

—Andy Chaleff, Author of *The Last Letter*

"This book really impacted my life. Being a recovering addict who put her mother through hell and back as well, this was a painful reminder of how much pain I caused. Thank you for reminding me of the many reasons why a day at a time I choose to stay in recovery even after seventeen years clean. I never want to go back to active addiction again.

—Marsha Rene, Author of *Silencing the Enemy Within Memoir of Addiction and Healing*

"In *Wake Up, Mom! Can't You See Your Son Is an Addict*, Linda Lee Henderson openly shares much of her adult life story and the pain, disappointment, anxiety, and heartbreak that became all too commonplace as she dealt with her son, who is an addict. Amazingly, her relentless persistence, resilience, and motherly love along with the help of professional counseling and rehabilitation services enabled her son to eventually find his purpose and place in life. A riveting read that I would highly recommend for any adult wishing to learn more about addictive behaviors."

—Bud Boughton, Author of *The Missing Piece*

"*Wake Up Mom!* is a heartbreaking story revealing the emotional seesaw a mother experiences in dealing with her son's addiction. It chronicles their lives as they live through his downward spiral. It is a must-read for any parent about to give up on their child.

—Joanne McCallie, Author of *Secret Warrior*

"In Linda Lee Henderson's riveting memoir, *Wake Up, Mom: Can't You See Your Son Is An Addict,* about the addiction of her son, Dana Henderson, and she and her daughter's own entanglement in his nearly twenty-year reliance on prescription drugs, Henderson's anguish and involvement in her attempts to come to the rescue of Dana is both harrowing and frustrating. *That's what moms do* is a constant refrain throughout this very readable memoir, and her redoubtable determination to help heal her son is at the very center of her difficult journey. One of the remarkable parts of this memoir is Henderson's willpower to function in the diurnal rhythms of life. Henderson is an adventurous woman, and her excursion from countries in South America, and from Pennsylvania, New Jersey, and the Outer Banks of North Carolina with stops in Prague and Paris make her memoir a reminder that the most profound obstacles on one's path in life can still have extremely rewarding moments. Without spoiling the ending of this wonderful memoir, it is safe to say Henderson's strength as a woman and mother propel this story to an important conclusion. I highly recommend reading this valuable memoir for both pleasure and instruction."

—Gerald L. Dodge, Author of *Beneath the Weight of Sadness*

"As a single mother of an adult child struggling with substance abuse, I found Linda's book spoke directly to me. Her estimate of the emotional, physical, and financial burden of supporting a child with an addiction is right on the mark. Yet her tireless self-examination, rationalization, misplaced assumptions, and guilt can be shared with any mother who has bought into the myth that moms are supposed to 'fix' anything that goes wrong in our families. Linda's is an amazing story of not just a mother's tenacity, but the triumph of the human spirit over the unforeseeable. As both a 'how to' and a 'how NOT to do' template, Linda's book is like looking in a mirror."

—Caroline McVitty, Retired Philadelphia Corporate Attorney and Former Feature Writer for a Suburban Daily Newspaper, Author of Movie-Review Blog at *McVittymovies.wordpress.com*

"As a friend I wish I could have been more help to Linda on her journey. Every journey through the disease of addiction is different and complicated. Words cannot express my joy for her and for Dana at his point in their lives. Recovery takes so much discipline and is not guaranteed. We all need others in a big way . . . not to do the work but to keep balanced. We all go off the rails. Linda saved Dana's life. My wife saved mine. *Wake Up, Mom* is a story that Linda shares in dramatic personal detail. As Linda shares: addiction is 'like a splinter in my soul constantly hurting and refusing to go away.'"

—Andy Kohlhepp, Licensed Professional Counselor, South Carolina Certified Addictions Counselor, Nationally Certified Counselor

Wake Up, Mom
Can't You See Your Son Is an Addict?

by Linda Lee Henderson

© Copyright 2021 Linda Lee Henderson

ISBN 978-1-64663-411-8

Published by

 köehlerbooks™

3705 Shore Drive
Virginia Beach, VA 23455
800-435-4811
www.koehlerbooks.com

WAKE UP, MOM

CAN'T YOU SEE YOUR SON IS AN ADDICT?

LINDA LEE HENDERSON

VIRGINIA BEACH
CAPE CHARLES

DEDICATION

THIS BOOK IS dedicated to all the families who have experienced the painful journey of the addiction of a loved one. Their lives have been forever changed.

It is also dedicated to those friends who helped me the most during my own arduous journey. Without their support and friendship, the journey would have been much harder to endure. Thank you, Kathy Buontempo, Dotty Crotty, and Maggie Kaye! You all listened to my tales and troubles and were always there to lend a helping hand. And a special thanks to my dear friend Chris Kolhepp, who unfortunately will never get to read my story. She has already found a special place in heaven.

I extend a huge emotional thank you to my two beautiful daughters, Julina and Shanna, who helped me navigate these challenging waters for so many years. Without their support I don't think I could have made it.

Lastly, a special thank you to all those who emotionally supported my son during all these years! There is a special place in heaven for you as well!

TABLE OF CONTENTS

PROLOGUE

IN TRYING TO figure out why I am writing this story to begin with, I have had to ask myself a lot of questions. Perhaps most of all: Am I writing this to help others or to help myself? I guess it's a little bit of both. This is a story about my son. And it is about a mother who is trying to figure out how everything went so wrong. My son, who was doing so well as a young boy, an adolescent, and then as a young man, slipped away from me, from us, and from reality. This is a story of his struggles for the past sixteen years. His struggles became my struggles, and I am grappling with a way to make sense of it all.

In telling Dana's story I have forced myself to examine every issue and every incident which may have influenced the outcome. I'm trying to piece together my life as a mom as well as Dana's in an effort to make sense of it all. In trying to understand if perhaps the dynamics of our family influenced the outcome, I've gone way back in time, before Dana was born. Originally, we were a cohesive though rather unconventional family. Our family unit unraveled, and I became a single mom. In trying to determine if I was caught up so much in my own life and struggles, I am forcing myself to relive those moments when I probably should have been more perceptive, more awake at the time. For a single mom trying to raise and educate three kids, life became a continual challenge. Every time it seemed

I had everything under control, an unforeseen incident would arise that would change everything.

Most of all, I need to try and determine why and how I missed the signs which eventually indicated his life was about to take a downward spiral. My two hopes are that perhaps I will somehow miraculously find a reason for what happened, or that perhaps by relaying this story I can, even in the tiniest way, help another family to recognize what I didn't see.

CHAPTER 1

MAY 2004

AT THE TIME, I thought it was the longest car trip of my life. I couldn't even speak. I just sat there numb—depressed and numb. My heart was aching, and my head was pounding. I was angry. I was disappointed and I was so, so sad. Wretchedly sad. I couldn't stop the flow of tears and grabbed for more tissues. I fingered the dress I was wearing, thinking that it was such a waste. I'd never wear it again. This couldn't have happened to me, to us. I kept reliving the events of the past 24 hours. Was it seriously just twenty-four hours ago?

Yesterday I was an elated mom. I was looking forward to my entire family gathering for the weekend at my son's college for his graduation. He is the youngest, Dana. His two sisters, Julina and Shanna, having already achieved that goal, were coming with their boyfriends. His grandparents were driving up from North Carolina, a lengthy road trip for them as his college, Union College, was in upper New York State. Even his father, whom I had divorced eleven years prior, was traveling up from Florida for this major event. Our plan for the day included a party with many of the families of his fraternity brothers, followed by a dinner with some of Dana's high school friends. The dinner was scheduled to take place at a lovely historic inn where we had made reservations months ahead. Everyone was looking forward to a glorious weekend.

I couldn't wait until Sunday. The graduation was to take place on Sunday morning on the quad of the campus. We were all going to meet early after breakfast and take a stroll around the campus to enjoy its eight acres of beautiful formal gardens and visit the famed Nott Memorial. It was to be a relaxing way to start the day. I was looking forward to that, as well as to the anticipation of finally achieving some economic relief. No more college bills, tuition, housing, or meal plans! Every parent of a college student looks forward to that moment. But very few parents experience what I experienced on that long-awaited day.

The weekend began on a non-momentous note. It was a beautiful spring morning as I set out on the drive to Dana's campus with my then-boyfriend Joe, whom I had been dating for about three years. I had splurged on a lovely spring dress for this special occasion.

We arrived on campus and Dana was nowhere to be found. My in-laws (I divorced their son, not them), were deep in conversation with Dylan, my ex, when we arrived. Introductions were made. It was a little awkward, but this wasn't about me or my ex or anything else. I could tell we were all of the same mindset regarding the weekend. Let's just get along and enjoy the experience for Dana's sake.

Dylan had not had much communication with Dana during the entire time our son was in college. An occasional email or phone call here and there and that's about it. Dylan had moved to Florida, and only came up to New Jersey to visit the kids for major events. I had been the one to cheer Dana on in his athletic ventures throughout high school and college. I was, in true fashion, a single mom. I was responsible for all and any decisions and did not consult Dylan on nearly anything. In hindsight, that was probably not the best decision. But we learn our fallacies only when we get older and see the results of our flawed judgments.

The conversation that morning eventually came around to what

Dana could possibly be doing that was so important he had missed greeting his guests. Dylan said he had seen him earlier, but Dana had told him he had to go speak to a professor. I didn't think much of it at the time and started a conversation with Ruth and John, my in-laws, about what the various members of the family had been doing. Dylan and I had been married for twenty-three years prior to the divorce, so I was no stranger to the fact that Dylan, being the first of thirty-six grandchildren, had a lot of relatives (cousins, aunts, uncles, and whatever), and we got engrossed in sorting out everyone else's lives.

When Dana finally arrived, he was breathless and full of apologies that he had had to run a few errands before the party. After greeting everyone and exchanging hugs, he led us over to an immense outdoor tent. We were to begin there the celebration of graduation weekend. We were a party of 10: Julina, my oldest daughter, and her then-boyfriend Russ; Shanna, my other daughter and her then-boyfriend/now-husband Mike; Dylan, Ruth and John, Dana, Joe, and myself. As we gathered under the tent, festively decorated with lights and filled with parents, would-be graduates, loud music, laughter, and noise, Dana pointed to a screen and told us to try and get a good view because there was to be a DVD show created by one of his friends, capturing college moments and memories.

As we all crowded in, I noticed that Dana seemed a bit on edge. I thought it was because all the family was finally there together, and he had no idea how that was going to play out. Granted, "grandparents meet mom's new boyfriend" could be a bit awkward, but so far we were fine, all getting along famously. We turned our attention to the screen, which was showing a myriad of pictures of his friends taken during their four years of college together. The DVD that was playing had been set to *Good Riddance*, the Green Day song that has become so popular at graduations and proms. *An excellent choice for a momentous occasion*, I thought. All of his friends were singing enthusiastically, while waving their beer steins in the air, "I hope you had the time of your life . . . ."

Today when I hear that song I am reminded of that day and the emotions it evoked. I felt pride as a single mother who had successfully navigated the financial waters of paying her son's way through school. I was delighted with Dana's accomplishment of finally reaching the end of the college education he had worked so hard for. I noted the number of friends he had there with him that glorious afternoon and thought, *Wow! He should be so happy right now.*

But I could tell he wasn't. Sensing something was wrong, I asked him about it.

"It's nothing, Mom. I'm fine. I'm glad everyone is here. But there's something else I have to do before we go to dinner tonight, so I'll be back in about half an hour. Why don't you all just stay here and enjoy yourselves and I'll catch up with you in a little bit."

With that, he was off. John made some joke about it being last-minute jitters, not unlike an imminent wedding. But I could tell something was off. They played the video again and this time I was not quite sure if this was in fact the time of his life.

Eventually we all made our way back to the nearby hotel where we were staying for the weekend. After a day of traveling, roaming around the campus, and partying, we wanted to freshen up for dinner. We went our separate ways and agreed to meet at the restaurant.

Finally dressed, at 6 p.m. we headed down toward the historic district of the city to the Stockade Inn restaurant, where the dinner was to be held. It was a beautiful venue with lots of old-world charm. I gazed around, taking in the beautiful oak ceilings, wainscoting, and soft lighting from the gas lamps flanking the walls. Off to the right, a table had been set for twenty-six people. That was our table. It extended clear from one end of the room to the other. This was perfect. We all chose our seats, with the boys choosing to sit with their respective families. I sat next to Dana, who remained quieter than normal throughout the meal. His behavior in no way indicated an enthusiasm one would expect from a young man about to graduate from college the next day. While this was out of character for him, I attributed his unusual behavior to nerves.

I was distracted from my concern as several of the other graduates gave rousing speeches, and the boys were applauded and toasted loudly many times. At about 11:00, we all agreed we'd had enough to eat and drink. It was getting late, so we all headed back to our rooms to get some rest for the next day.

SUNDAY A.M.

It was 6:00 and my cell phone was ringing. *What an ungodly time to call and talk*, I thought. I answered, and it was Dana.

"Mom, I really need to talk to you. It's important."

"Dana, I'm not even up yet! Can this wait? It's six a.m.! What's wrong?"

"I just need to talk to you. Just meet me outside your room in fifteen minutes. I'm going to walk over there. And don't tell anyone else, OK?"

"Dana? What is going on?"

"*Mom*! Just meet me, OK?" And with that he hung up. I looked over at Joe, who by now was awake.

"What's going on?" he asked.

I shook my head. "I have no idea, but he sounds really upset. He wants me to meet him outside in fifteen minutes. I don't know what to think!"

"OK, just try and stay calm. Get dressed and go see what he wants."

I threw on some clothes (not my expensive "graduation dress") and ran outside to meet Dana. He was already waiting for me, pacing. Dana was always pacing, He had Attention Deficit Hyperactive Disorder (ADHD) and we always joked about whenever he became nervous he would pace around my center kitchen island in rapid circles as he tried to make a point. This time he was uncharacteristically upset.

"Dana, tell me. What is going on?"

"Mom, I don't know how to tell you this. I've been up all night. I haven't slept a bit. You're going to be really upset and I'm really sorry, but I am not walking today."

"What do you mean you're not walking?"

"I'm not going to graduate today! That's what I mean!"

"What?! Why not?!"

"It's all a mess! I tried talking to one of my professors, but I couldn't find him yesterday. I was told the other day I didn't have enough credits."

"How could you not know this?" I cried.

"Mom, it's just all a mess. The credits I took at Union County College didn't get on my transcript and I've been trying all week to fix this but now it's too late and no one is around to help me."

"Well, if you have the credits and they are just not on your transcript you should walk anyway. This can all be fixed later. Everyone has come up here to see you graduate. You can't disappoint them!"

"Mom, I know! You think I don't feel terrible about this?! And especially Grandma and Granddad! I told them last night, actually. I went to their room after dinner and they give me a graduation gift and a beautiful blanket from the college here, and I just had to tell them. I can't walk if they are not going to announce my name!"

"Dana, you need to just get yourself together. If you don't walk you are going to regret it for the rest of your life. Go back to your room and get yourself ready. You need to do this!"

"Mom! I can't! I don't want to! Look, I need you to tell Dad. He's going to be really upset with me."

"Well *I'm* upset with you! Never mind, I'll call him. Go back to your room and we'll sort this out."

That's what mothers do. They sort things out. At this point I was thinking that if I couldn't persuade him myself, perhaps we could all go over to his room together, as a family, and persuade him to walk. I needed time to think.

The next hour or so is a total blur in my mind. Not because it was sixteen years ago, but because I was so drastically upset I couldn't think straight. I remember calling Dylan and then the girls, telling them the turn of events and that they should meet me at Dana's room in an hour at the house he was renting with some friends. Surely we could talk him into walking. I would have John talk to him. He always listened to his Granddad. Somewhat optimistically, I showered and donned my expensive going-to-graduation dress.

Joe and I arrived shortly after the others. I saw immediately that Julina and Russ, Shanna and Mike, and Ruth and John were already on the front porch when we finally found a parking spot. None of them looked very happy. They were all talking quietly.

"John," I asked as I approached, "do you think you could talk to Dana and persuade him to walk? He always listens to you."

"Well, Linda," he replied, "I have already been up there and I don't think he's going to change his mind."

"Maybe we should all go up there," I cried in desperation. "He has to walk!"

John shook his head. "You can try," he answered calmly, "but I don't think he needs a group of us up there right now. He is pretty upset."

OK then. Me being me, I marched upstairs, only to find his room in total chaos, Dana not showered or dressed, but lying in a heap on his bed sobbing.

"Dana, really! Everyone is downstairs waiting for you! You have to get showered and dressed. You have to walk. We'll sort out the rest later."

I frantically searched his room for his cap and gown, throwing things everywhere in the process.

"Dana! Come on! Where is your cap and gown?"

He just looked at me. "Mom, I don't have them. I never picked them up."

At that point, I just collapsed in a chair. The realization that my son was not going to graduate dawned. Numbly, I got up and walked out of his disheveled room. What the hell just happened?

As I made my way downstairs, I could hear bagpipes in the distance warming up for the graduation festivities. Back on the porch, we all stood there and looked at one another. Talking about this wasn't going to help. We all looked over at John when he said, "Well, folks, I think the best thing to do right now is get off the campus and go somewhere for breakfast. I'll go get Dana and tell him we're getting him away from this place for the morning."

And that's what we did. We took our party of ten to breakfast rather than to graduation.

But the ugliest chapter of my life story had just begun on that fated non-graduation day. The day I considered the worst of my life was to be followed by many more. What ensued was mostly caused by factors out of my control. Or was it? The signs and the patterns were there. Either I didn't see them or I chose not to.

This story is about sixteen years of pain. It is about how one well-meaning psychiatrist, in prescribing a study drug to my son, managed to turn his life upside-down. It is about how a once bright, athletic young man has now undergone multiple surgeries, has been hospitalized at least a dozen times, and has been in rehab three times. It is about how my son literally has been fighting for his life every day for sixteen years. It is about the emotional, physical, and financial toll it has had on all of us. No family should ever have to experience this. But we have, and I want to share it with you.

CHAPTER 2

JANUARY 1, 2020
STARTING TO PUT THINGS IN ORDER

ON THE FIRST day of this new year, I was having my morning coffee, scrolling through my Facebook page. Someone (an anonymous author) had posted a very clever summation of life's answered questions. Upon reading it, I was amused and found it particularly so since, like the author of the post, I had just turned seventy. Thinking I could make someone else's day brighter and make them laugh, I decided to send it on to twenty or so friends. While it seemed like a good idea at the time, some were ticked off as I sent it via a group text. As a result, many phones were blowing up all morning. I won't do that again. (But, I was rewarded with many "laugh until I cry" emojis.)

I'll share it with you. (I wish I had written this. It's clever!)

"It's the year 2020. I'm seventy years old and still have so many unanswered questions. I haven't found out who let the dogs out . . . where's the beef . . . how to get to Sesame Street . . . why Dora just doesn't use Google Maps . . . Why do all the flavors of Fruit Loops taste exactly the same, or how many licks does it take to get to the center of a Tootsie Pop . . . why eggs are packaged in a flimsy carton, but batteries are secured in plastic that's tough as nails . . . what does the fox say

. . . why "abbreviated" is such a long word, or why there is a D in 'fridge' but not refrigerator . . . why lemon juice is made with artificial flavor yet dishwashing liquid is made with real lemon juice . . . why you put your two cents in" but it's only "a penny for your thoughts"--where's that extra penny going . . . why does the "Alphabet Song" and "Twinkle Twinkle Little Star" have the same tune . . . why did you just try to sing those two previous songs,.and just what exactly is Victoria's secret? And where is Waldo?"

After I read this I thought, *Right! But he or she forgot, "why do you drive on a parkway, but park in a driveway*?

OK, I thought. *Haven't you got anything better to do with your life? How about your own unanswered questions? Why don't you try and make sense of them? Why don't you try and figure out your own life and Dana's and the twists and turns that you both have experienced?* I had been thinking about this a lot recently. Maybe I should try and write down my story.

I have always loved to read. I have read voraciously since the time I was young. Starting with the Bobbsey Twins, Nancy Drew, the Hardy Boys, all the fairy tales by the Brothers Grimm, my much-treasured biographies of famous people, then moving on to whatever was available when the bookmobile came to town. I was in seventh heaven in college when we were required to read *War and Peace*, as it was one of my favorites. As an adult I download at least one or two books a week. I love to read but never had the aspiration to write. Some do; I never did.

But that New Year's morning, I realized that I had to do that. I had to write this story down. Doing that would force me to look back and try and make sense out of all that had happened. I needed to go back and try and figure out if somehow our own family history played a part in the events that were to follow. I needed to see what role I had played in this, if any. Maybe the blame ultimately lay with me. Was this problem exacerbated because I was a single parent? These were questions that had been in my mind for years. It is a painful thought when I realize that so many incidents might have been avoided if I had just paid attention to the signs. Now, years later, I was going to try and figure out how I might have determined when everything was going to fall apart. It is much too late to have prevented the outcome, but maybe the reexamination of events would help me to make sense of it.

Having decided to tackle this project, I needed to figure out a way to remember all that had preceded. I hadn't kept a diary of any of the events. But so many memories had just kept replaying in my head for years like a bad recurring dream. I most likely had blocked out many events. But somehow the worst ones were right there on the surface, like a splinter in my soul, constantly hurting and refusing to go away. Maybe writing this story would help remove the splinter. Perhaps my tale could even help others recognize signs that indicate their children's problems are deeper than they suspect.

To begin, I needed to examine my life and the family Dana was born into. Every family is unique. Ours certainly was and still is. Multiple moves and unsettling events are bound to have an impact on any family. To say I faced challenges in my life as a young married woman would be an understatement. These challenges would set the tone for the independent mom I became—perhaps too independent. When we finally moved back to the United States, after living in South America for ten years, I perhaps gained a false sense of security. Then our family unraveled. Once I became a single mom, I spent my life trying to be the best mother ever by providing for my children. I also spent my life trying to fix problems instead of trying to understand them. Maybe that was the problem.

When people hear that a son or daughter has a problem in life it is common to immediately point a finger at the parents. They are judged. Their lives are examined. I have tried to examine ours to see if our lifestyle or decisions were somehow related to Dana's issues. We started out as a normal family, sort of. My daughters believe otherwise. They call it a dysfunctional family. You can decide for yourself.

While putting downs these thoughts and recollections I realized I have bits of paper, memos, calendars, pictures, you name it, everywhere. It occurred to me that it was as if I were trying to put together a puzzle. I would seize upon something that happened and think, *That's it! Why didn't I see that before?*

I told a friend about this and he advised me, "Be careful. Go ahead and try and do it, but when it's all done, and the puzzle is all together, you may not like what you see."

I knew he might be right, but that I was going to try not to leave anything out. I would let the complete picture tell the story.

I started to write this story nearly a decade ago—when I thought I could close the final chapter. But then all seemed well with Dana and the world, and why dredge up old memories best left forgotten? The book disappeared in my old computer and I couldn't retrieve it. *Let it be!* I told myself. I was hoping I would never have cause to finish it. But I did.

When I finally decided to resurrect the project, I knew I would have to start from scratch. It would be painful, and it's difficult to reconstruct events from jumbled memories. However, I did discover one thing. I did have a thread of all that had happened, and it was right in my desk all along—sixteen years of checkbooks. For some reason I had kept every one. Realizing that, I knew I did have a sort of diary of all that had happened—every single check I had written for Dana's life journey during that time. I then spent days going through those checkbooks and listing, month by month and year by year, the money I had invested in my son. In doing so I realized there was a pattern. If I had learned nothing else, I learned this. I should have seen that pattern in black and white, laid out in front of me years ago. Not that it would have averted some events, but more so that I could have perhaps foreseen what was coming.

CHAPTER 3

1974—OUR EARLY BEGINNINGS AS PARENTS

OUR LIVES AS a married couple up to the point of Dana's birth had been anything but normal. As a military family until 1971 and then as expats, we had already relocated nine times in our eight years of marriage. It seemed normal at the time. I used to say that we lived our lives "backwards" from most people. Because of the locales we were assigned to, we had household help as it was financially feasible and much needed in places like Bangkok, where we didn't even have a washer or dryer. Because of Dylan's assignments, we were able to travel extensively. Some people wait their entire lives to be able to do what we were doing in our twenties. There were many external factors affecting our lives and determining the people we would become. Events that I promise you I am not making up.

Dylan and I had been in search of a stone home in 1974. We both liked the idea of stability and that seemed to offer us the best option. We had moved to Pennsylvania from Virginia where both of us had recently obtained our master's degrees from The College William and Mary after finishing our stint in the military. Dylan was newly employed at a large industrial gas company in Trexelertown. For the first six months we rented an apartment in Bethlehem. He worked and I taught a bilingual first grade class at Donegan Elementary School in Bethlehem, which was comprised mostly of students of Bethlehem Steel employees.

After six months in our tiny apartment, we aggressively began the search for our first home. After several months and several calls to my dad to come over from New Jersey to assess our potential purchase, he and Dylan and I agreed we had found the perfect property. It was a converted stone barn on 10 acres. In 1974 the asking price was $60,000, a lot of money at that time. The required down payment to get a loan was thirty percent. The economy was not great, but we had been working and saving for five years. As we had spent a year in Thailand, Dylan at U-Tapau Air Force Base and me in Bangkok teaching at the International School, we had lived for practically nothing. We had money saved for just this purpose, so we made an offer. Shockingly, ours was met with a competing offer. Yes, even then the aggravating bidding wars existed. Thankfully, the home's owner liked us and agreed to sell to us.

As the new owners, we began making great plans for our new dream home. We worked long and hard on improvements. We wanted to put in a pond, add another garage, and expand the living area. But, alas, that wasn't to be. The company decided that Dylan was the perfect choice to work in the financial sector of their Brazilian operation located in Sao Paulo. Dylan had once lived in Spain, spoke perfect Spanish, and I was a Spanish major. Apparently, his bosses failed to recognize that Portuguese, not Spanish, is the language of Brazil. Close enough, right?

After much discussion, we decided to accept the "exploratory tour" trip offered by the company, to see if in fact Sao Paulo was a place we could live. I was expecting our first child at the time and this was no easy task for a mama-to-be. We stayed for about a week with another couple, Moe and Candy, who were terrific hosts. They were ex pats, had a child, and had been there for two years already. Candy taught me several things about Brazil during that trip.

First of all, Brazil at that time was a country in which families with any kind of means had to have nannies for their children. There were no disposable diapers, no prepared baby foods, no babysitters or services, and kitchens didn't come with appliances. The minimal appliances were purchased by the landlord of the property because the women didn't cook. There were maids to do that. If you owned any convenience appliances you better bring them with you because Brazil didn't have them. And if you wanted any kind of sound system, bring that, too. Furniture and cars we could purchase, but bring maple syrup, as there was none of that to be had.

Having gained all the necessary knowledge, we returned to the States and accepted the tour. Julina was due in November, and they wanted us to move the following March. She was to be only four months old when we relocated. *OK*, we decided, *no big deal*. But what to do with our stone house?

There was no way we were going to sell the home we had recently acquired and put so much work into during the year we had been there. So we decided to contact a local real estate agent and offer the property for rent. Because our property was located a good half-hour from a town of any substantial size, she decided to advertise it as "total seclusion." A tenant was found and a lease was drawn up. We were on our way to Brazil.

So began our life and routine in Brazil. I worked at Graded School teaching first grade, at first only half days. This is when I first met Joyce Pickering and began my training with her. I shared the teaching of a first-grade class with "Mary," a woman who would become a good friend. She and her husband "Peter" would join us many times for dinner. After the meal, in one corner Mary and I would rehash events of our teaching day and in the other Dylan and Peter would speak quietly for hours. We were too busy in our own conversation to pay any heed to their discussion.

As both Dylan and I were working, we found a nanny for Julina. After all, someone had to boil the diapers and make the baby food.

She was a Paulista, that is, a person from Sao Paulo. About four years my younger, she seemed mature enough to handle a young baby. She had had experience working for another family who had to relocate. Her name was Dina.

Our home was located on a cobblestone street near Iguatami Shopping Center on Rua Travesa Oro Preto, where I took Julina for walks in her umbrella stroller. Nearly anywhere I went, I walked. I did not drive at all for the first six months there. It was too unnerving. If I went anywhere in the car, Mary drove. She had already been living there for three years and was comfortable navigating the crazy traffic. We didn't have many visitors from the States. It was an eleven-hour plane ride and the family couldn't seem to find the time or the money for the expensive airfare.

We did have visitors from the home company. One such person was Dan, Dylan's boss in the US. After we had been in Sao Paulo for about five months, Dan came down and we had him over to dinner. I remember running out of propane that night and trying in a panic to figure out what to serve. This young bride didn't want to make a bad impression. After dinner, which turned out to be creative sandwiches, we asked if he could please drive to our stone house when he returned home and make sure everything was alright. We were anxious because we had put so much into it and wanted to make sure everything was OK on the home front. He agreed. No problem.

The "seclusion" of our home in Pennsylvania started with a driveway that was about a third of mile long and wound down into a deeply wooded area. It was impossible to see the home from the street or any neighboring property. Dan knew where the house was located as he had had dinner there with us on more than one occasion while trying to persuade us to accept the Brazilian assignment. Upon his return from Sao Paolo, he dutifully headed there to check on it for us.

As he approached the end of the driveway, he noticed that it had a large chain across secured with a padlock. *That's really peculiar,* he thought as he peered down the tree-topped driveway. Seeing no one, he parked his car and headed off down the lane. As he neared the house he noticed that my previously lovely flower gardens had been woefully unattended, and there were very large plants growing alongside the driveway near the house. He knocked at the door, but no one answered. Seeing that the house was still intact if not well cared for, he reported back to us. He mentioned the abandoned gardens and large plants and told us about the strange chain and padlock.

A few days later we received a large envelope via courier company mail, which is how we always corresponded with those back in the States, company members and family alike. In it was the front page of the *Reading News* with a picture of our home on the front page, with the headline, "LARGEST DRUG BUST IN PENNSYLVANIA HISTORY."

Well, this was quite a bombshell! Clearly, we had not chosen the perfect renters. In reading the article we discovered that our tenants, who had been so interested in privacy, were in fact not only growing marijuana on our property but using the garage for a storage facility. Apparently, the shipments were being brought in from Mexico. Our lovely stone house had now become a drug distribution center.

It was also reported to us that the police may have some questions for us. Perhaps there was a Brazilian connection? They had discovered that we had rented out the house and were living in Brazil. Oh, and did I mention that Dylan used to have a large gun collection? The guns were placed for safe keeping with a friend before we went overseas. However, in the basement he had a very large cabinet of ammunition which he decided to leave in the house. The police, upon discovering this cabinet in their raid on our once-lovely home, had undertaken a zealous search for the guns which they assumed were in the house. It was reported to us that they had gone up into the attic and ripped out all the insulation in their search. We were pretty pissed at the entire situation and decided that we needed to go back to Pennsylvania to assess the damage. Oh, and find another tenant as our current one was now in jail.

So, a trip was planned. In 1976 airlines allowed travelers to go from point A to point B with as many additional stops as one wanted along the way. Since we were young and wanted to visit other countries, we decided to find at least some good in the distressful situation and do some traveling on our return trip to the US. We decided on Machu Picchu.

Living overseas had its advantages despite its many trials. We were fortunate to have already made many friends in Sao Paulo. Since we now spoke Portuguese as well as Spanish, we were able to strike up friendships with people who otherwise would have been strangers in our midst. One family, related to a co-worker of Dylan's, invited us to visit them in their hometown in La Paz, Bolivia. So we decided to start there and then continue to Peru. Julina was not old enough to walk yet, but we would manage. Ah, youth!

That eventful trip stays in my mind for so many reasons. Getting off the plane in La Paz, which has an altitude of over 13,000 feet, and getting the headache of my life was the first one. However, our friends had the instant remedy for this and rapidly gave us coca tea, which instantly did the trick. . Our voyage across the reflective waters of Lake Titicaca and taking in the spectacular view of the Andes Mountains was another special moment. On the hydrofoil we befriended another American couple also making their way to the ruins. Upon our arrival in Puno on the Peruvian side, we all traveled by bus to Cusco, from where we would depart to Machu Picchu. Upon arrival, we checked into a modest hotel, located right in the downtown. The next day we were to make our way by train up the mountain to the ancient ruins.

As a seasoned traveler I can truthfully say that the breathtaking view we saw when we first rounded the hill and saw the Incan ruins was one of most powerful moments I ever experienced. The panoramic views and abandoned city captivated us from the first glimpse. We were fortunate to be able to easily navigate around all the ruins in just a few hours. In 1976 this was not a popular destination. There was no "Trip Advisor." There was no internet. There was just a *Frommer's Travel Guide* advising us where to go, how to get there and where to stay. There maybe were ten to twenty other families up there with us. We took enough pictures to be able to successfully bore all family members whom we could persuade to sit through our slide shows and headed back to Cusco on the train.

Upon arrival at our hotel, we immediately noticed many disturbances in the street. This was disappointing as we had been anticipating wandering around the streets of this capital of the Cusco Province in the hope of capturing yet more photographs. We started to plan our next walking adventure as we stood in front of our hotel. Instead, at the entrance we were shepherded inside and haltingly (in English, so there was no misunderstanding) told to stay off the streets as there was fighting going on. A revolution had begun. You didn't have to tell me twice. I fled up to the room with Julina, and of course Dylan headed out the door in hopes of capturing on film some historic moments. An opportunity not to be missed! Hours later, as I was on my knees giving Julina a bath in the tub, he arrived panting, recounting what he had seen and the photos he had taken.

"Dylan," I said calmly, "I can see what is going on in the streets below. We need to make plans to leave immediately. It's dangerous and this is no place for anyone, let alone a baby!"

He agreed and went down to the front desk to make a plan for ourselves and our new friends to leave the hotel under the cover of darkness. We left quietly out the back door of the hotel at 3 a.m. The hotel had a taxi waiting, which drove us quickly to the airport. Our plane wasn't to depart until 7 a.m. We now were headed to Bogota, Colombia, because that is where the earliest plane was headed. We were shocked when we arrived at the airport. Hundreds of visitors were arriving on flights with the intent to head up to Machu Picchu. Apparently, no one advised them of the revolution.

Thankfully, our flight to Bogota was uneventful except for the fact that, in our haste, we realized that we had left Julina's beloved "blankie" in the hotel in Cusco. The one she couldn't sleep without. Next quest for us was to find a place to sleep in Bogota. We hadn't planned that stop. Four decades later, I can't recall the name of the hotel. But our friends recommended the nicest one downtown and we headed there. We arrived dirty, disheveled, and with a crying baby. Dylan explained to the manager what we had just experienced and, just like that, we were given the Presidential Suite at the rate of a single room. All was now good with the world. We explored Bogota for a few days, then decided to head to Caracas, Venezuela. It was the logical choice. We needed to get to a city that had direct departures for the US. And our new friends had friends who lived in Caracas, so why not?

A simple departure from Bogota wasn't in the cards. It was customary for the officials to take your passports when you checked in and then return them to the passengers as they boarded the flight. We complied. Upon the return of the officials, however, we had two passports, not three. Julina's had somehow "gone missing." And that, folks, is how some illegal passports are obtained. Her four-month baby picture could have been any baby. Obtaining these illegally acquired passports by the Colombian officials was obviously a side business of theirs, selling them to the highest bidder. Somewhere in the world is another child with the same name as my daughter. We were allowed on the plane. Apparently a four-month-old baby is no threat. But only after the same officious characters had painstakingly gone through her baby cereal to ascertain there were no hidden drugs in it.

That was our first trip to Caracas, to which we would relocate many years later. I was immediately impressed with its beautiful weather and Romanesque architecture. The people were amazingly friendly and we spent an interesting two days there exploring the city while awaiting our flight. The US flights then were all scheduled for the early morning. Caracas is situated in a mountain valley some 3,000 feet above sea level and was about an hour drive to the airport, so we arose quite early. Having successfully obtained a taxi, we said goodbye to all our new friends and headed out. About halfway there, on a winding mountain road, the taxi driver suddenly gunned the motor and took off at a terrifying speed. Of course, I screamed. Suddenly he slowed down and stopped and looked back. Not realizing what had happened, I looked back, too. We had very, very narrowly avoided a rock avalanche. Fortunately, he had seen it start as we were already in its path. Once through it, we all realized the road was now no longer passable. Holding my baby tightly in my arms, shaking, I realized what could have happened. What a trip! First a revolution, a stolen passport, and now an avalanche. This was not a trip for the faint of heart.

We forged ahead to the airport. It was time to get back to the States and see what more good news awaited us with regards to our stone house. Our return flight to the US was mostly empty. Not many had made it through that mountain pass earlier than us, and they subsequently all missed the flight. We received excellent service on the nearly empty plane. On the flight home we recalled our adventures. We thought we were quite clever for having coped with many unexpected challenges thrown at us. Those experiences led me to believe that as young parents we together were quite capable of dealing with the unexpected. But we were young, and time would prove that we were not as clever as we thought.

Once home in the US, we met with our neighbors and the police to get the real news of the now famous drug bust. After a lengthy discussion, the police finally determined that we had nothing to do with the mysterious arrival of a ton of marijuana to our garage. We were guilty of making a poor choice of a renter. You think? The state police, having had their suspicions of this unsavory character, had placed stakeouts in the woods around our home in their fervent attempt to catch him. This was a very rural area and several neighbors had, while hunting, surprisingly encountered the state police. The surveillance had apparently gone on for a few weeks. We didn't exactly get a welcoming party from the neighbors, who were never particularly friendly after that.

What did they do with the ton of confiscated marijuana, you might ask. Well, it wasn't disposed of instantly. There was a great deal of local discussion about how to dispose of it. It was later reported to us that the citizens of Reading, the nearest town of any size, refused to allow the authorities to dispose of it by burning it in the city's local dump. It was feared that everyone in the vicinity would get high. So, it was handily decided to truck it out somewhere in the country, dig a hole, and bury it—a great idea in theory. Unfortunately, though, the large truck that was hauling the confiscated pot got into an accident. The truck exploded and the marijuana flew everywhere. End of story. This, too, made the front page of the papers. We were becoming famous, and we didn't even live in the country. We managed to clean up the mess made by the tenants (and the police) and set about to find a new tenant.

Why am I relating all these seemingly unrelated stories? Good question. But reminiscing about such events reminds me that for years, while adversities were constantly thrown at us, Dylan and I managed just fine. While we had crazy events challenge our everyday life, we were able to cope with whatever situation challenged us. We were a team then, acting as one. This was not the case, years later, when we needed to act as a cohesive unit in regard to Dana.

CHAPTER 4

OUR "PERFECT" LIFE AS EXPATS

OUR FIRST BRAZILIAN tour lasted from 1976-1980. We tried to make the most of our stay in Sao Paulo. Part of the attraction in accepting an overseas assignment was to learn a new culture and a new language and have an opportunity to travel. During our time there we became friends with other expats who were living very similar lives to ours. Most of our leisure time was spent getting together with these families, especially on holidays, as our own families were so far away. We all became a very close-knit group. It was not unusual for fourteen of us to go out to dinner together, at about 10 p.m. as was the tradition. We entertained a lot, took in shows when there were any, and enjoyed camping trips to the uninhabited beaches between Sao Paulo and Rio de Janeiro (the current site of a large Club Med resort). We visited Belo Horizonte, Guaraja, and Ouro Preto—anywhere to escape the city. In 1976, some eleven million people (10 percent of Brazil's population) lived in Sao Paulo. Clear air was a rare commodity, and we took every opportunity to escape the pollution which constantly shrouded the city. As I mentioned, we had a nanny at that time. She sometimes accompanied us on our weekend retreats to take care of Julina. Bad idea.

While living there it was difficult to overlook the striking contrast between the extremely advantaged and disadvantaged people all living together in the chaos of the city. There essentially was no middle class. As expats we were somewhere in No Man's Land. Life was a challenge navigating through the busy streets trying to acquire weekly essentials or trying to get to work on time. Despite our many criticisms though, we did admire how the Brazilians recognized the importance of family and friends. The people more than made up for the horrible congestion of the city.

Much like any other family, we had our special friends as well. My best friend while living in Brazil was Sarah. Our husbands worked together and the four of us were inseparable. It was with them we often trekked off to find a beach on which to camp for the weekend. We would all wake up early, around 4 a.m., to pack the car with our essentials of tents, sleeping bags, water, food, and our favorite beverages. Add to this an inflatable boat, fishing gear, generators, and beach toys. The cars were laden and we strapped to the top whatever didn't fit in. Our small caravan left at that hour to avoid the horrific traffic. We would head down the mountain as the sun rose over the trees. We traveled down narrow rutted roads in pursuit of a deserted beach. We felt ourselves to be quite adventurous, although a little crazy. We would set up camp near whatever river we could find. Camping rustic-style, it wasn't unusual to be washing our dinnerware in the ocean only to have it swept away by an unanticipated large wave. At this, we would just shriek with laughter.

When we weren't setting out to a weekend destination, Sarah and I would get together in the evenings while our "boys" were out dining with clients or entertaining folks visiting from the States. We took up sewing and decided to make ourselves new outfits because what we were finding in Sao Paulo wasn't working. Sarah was always the fashionable one, with her dark hair, slender body, and sophisticated clothes. I think she was trying to encourage me to be a little less frumpy, which I most likely was. I had just had a baby and I needed an overhaul. We decided I needed a new hairdo as well. That didn't go well. After getting a perm, all the rage at the time, I took one look in the mirror and decided I needed to wear a hat that evening to a party they were hosting. Two weeks later I had it cut off. I tried.

Sarah and her husband had no children but desperately wanted a baby. They decided to adopt and put their names on a list as candidates for a child. Thinking it would take months or even a year for this to happen, they were shocked when after only four weeks they got the call. Sarah called me in disbelief.

"They have a baby for us! I can't believe it! I'm not ready! I don't have anything!"

"Oh my God," I cried. "When do you get it? Is it a boy or a girl?"

It was a boy and had been left at a hospital by the mother. They needed to go that evening and collect him. If the authorities came, they were to say it was left on their doorstep. And that is how adoption takes place in Brazil. When she explained that I was speechless. But now I had to get into action. After ending the call with her, I raced around my house collecting everything I had for a newborn baby, threw it all in the car, and headed for their apartment.

Moments like that you never forget. That child had to be the luckiest boy in Brazil. He was adopted by a loving, caring American family. He was born in the favellas, the slums of Sao Paulo. He would grow up in much more fortunate circumstances and later became one of my son's best friends.

When we did finally leave the "concrete jungle," as it was referred to, we would miss our friends the most. Our tour was up in 1980 and we returned to Pennsylvania. By this time my second daughter Shanna had been born, so we now returned with two young children. It was time to get our house straight and live normal lives. Dylan went to work and I got hepatitis. I guess we should have steered clear of that last beach hut we ate at in Guaraja. It was a great relief to now be able to call my mom to help me out because now she was only an hour's drive away, not eleven hours by plane. The hepatitis made me so weak it was an effort to lift a coffee cup. I had two little girls to take care of and was alone most of the time. Dylan wasn't around much as he was working in New Jersey and stayed there most of the week. I needed some assistance.

Hearing I was sick, Dylan's mother called and also offered to help. She decided to come up from North Carolina to help me with the kids because I was pretty useless in my weakened state. She had been there for about three days when I received the daily mail. In it was a letter from my friend Linda who was still living in Brazil. I made coffee for both of us and sat down at our kitchen table with my mother-in-law to read the letter. I was reading it aloud to Ruth when I got to a part about Dina, our former maid. I read ahead rapidly to myself and then stopped. Linda was writing to tell me that her own maid, who was best friends with Dina, had told her that Dina was pregnant, and that Senor Dylan was the father. Yep, that would be Dylan, my husband, father of my children. I paused then read and reread this to myself, and then stumbled through some excuse to stop reading. I don't think Ruth noticed my reaction. I was floored. My world had just fallen apart.

A few days later, when Dylan returned from New Jersey, I confronted him with this news. He said we would talk about it at dinner. He had some things to explain. No kidding! We went out to a local restaurant and talk we did. It was nothing, he said. No, he definitely wasn't the father. In fact, he told me he had already paid for Dina to have an abortion once because she slept around a lot. She had come to him for the money and he had given it to her to help her out. He hadn't wanted to tell me at the time. He then went on to say that it was in fact the accepted practice in Brazil for the men to have liaisons with the help. Seriously? He assured me it meant nothing and there was no way that he was the father. But, in fact, he was going to tell me about his short tryst with her anyway, he said, because we were actually in the process of trying to obtain a work visa for Dina to come to the States and help me. He had decided in light of the circumstances that probably wasn't a good idea. I tended to agree.

As if this recent revelation wasn't enough to rock my world, he also told me that he had gotten word that his new company wanted us to move back to Brazil. Oh, marvelous! Recognizing there was a never-ending grapevine of gossip in the expat community, I was finding it hard to envision returning to the scene of the crime, so to speak. How could I possibly move back there with him, knowing this? It wasn't like we were unknowns in the community. The person who spilled the beans was the maid of my former principal, for whom I would now be returning to work. My head was spinning. I needed to think, but he was still talking. In trying to explain it away, he assured me it was a one-night thing, and nothing like that had ever happened before and never would again. I wanted to believe him. I didn't want a divorce. I had two young children. I tried to put it behind me. I never shared that conversation with anyone until years later.

We stayed together. After much discussion, we decided he would accept the position in Brazil. We would be moving back to Sao Paulo. I had no idea what I was getting myself into and approached the move with a lot of trepidation. Even so, we began our plans to again relocate.

A week later I received a letter from Dina, who had gotten my address from Linda's maid. In the letter she begged me to send her money and clothes for the baby she was expecting. I answered her. I wrote a very long letter in Portuguese, explaining how that was so not going to happen, and we in fact were returning to Brazil and I wanted nothing to do with her. She needed to stay out of our lives. I needed to put an end to the whole thing. I was going to pretend it never happened. I had to believe Dylan. I was willing her out of my life. I had to concentrate on the move and my two daughters.

Upon leaving Brazil the prior year, we had had a huge sale, a liquidation sale of sorts, selling all our US possessions to those lucky ones who arrived early. They did arrive early, 6 a.m. to be exact. There was so much we were selling that was unattainable in the Brazilian market. As luck would have it, the very day we had our sale, a huge devaluation took place in the country. As we took in a lot of cash, it pretty much was instantly lost. "Good riddance," we had thought, "Enough of this place!" At that time I had no idea that the devaluation of the cruzeiro was probably not my greatest worry in the world.

In retrospect, I cannot believe we even considered returning. But once you are on the international circuit you pretty much have to go on the road, or you lose your place in line. So I knew that we would accept. I was trying to be a good wife. I also knew we were going to have to go through the laborious process of reacquiring, in a hurry, all that we had sold. Our intent initially was to do it slowly. But no, the company wanted us there as soon as possible. So again, movers were called and the house was rented out, again. And move we did.

For those who haven't had the pleasure of an international move, let me just say a lot of time is spent in hotels. Each time upon arrival, we were forced to spend six to eight weeks in a hotel "waiting for our shipment." All our worldly goods that weren't in storage were somewhere on a sea vessel, and it was somewhat unnerving to wait and see if they would arrive. I remember one family, upon departing Brazil, did not fare so well. Their container somehow slipped off the ship and lost everything they owned. I was so certain that was going to happen to us in light of other bad luck we had already experienced. Fortunately, it did not. We did, however, spend many, many weeks at the Hotel Cadoro. We stayed there so many times I lost track. Fortunately, we made many good friends there who were in the same situation. It became our second home.

So, we moved back to the Hotel Cadoro where the staff, now well known to us, greeted us with open arms. We were back to waiting for our shipment and back to our lives in Brazil. Shanna, who was turning three, had a very elaborate birthday party there, the likes of which she would never see again. I spent an inordinate amount of time searching for a new home that would suit my acceptance and the budget the company had set. I finally found one in Morumbi, close to the school where the girls would attend and where I would return to teach. I was nervous about returning to the school and finding out whatever the grapevine had revealed.

Dina, the pregnant maid, did appear on our doorstep upon our arrival, begging for her job back. Dylan met with her and told her no way and to go away. She didn't. She called the house so many times we finally had to have the phone number changed. Thus began our new lives in Brazil.

CHAPTER 5

BRAZIL 1981 . . . A NEW ARRIVAL

OUR "TRANQUIL" FAMILY history set the scene for our new arrival. This was the family my son was born into. I found out in September I was pregnant with Dana. Having sold all my baby apparatus prior to our departure from Sao Paulo six months before, I was ill equipped for this. I had nothing. Fortunately, Sarah still had much of what I had lent to her and we had other friends with young children. By April, I had acquired a crib, play pen, highchair, and a walker. I begged my mother to send me a pad for the changing table, baby washcloths, undershirts, and diaper pins. It seemed I was always sick. The smell of fish made me gag and I had toast every day. The skies were constantly grey, as only Sao Paulo can be in winter, and I suffered my third cold during my pregnancy. None of this made me feel attractive.

We also found out in September we had a problem with our new tenants renting our Pennsylvania home. In an effort to find a law-abiding citizen to rent our property, before leaving to return to Brazil, we decided to place an ad in the paper, not mentioning complete privacy. This was a local couple, however, who were familiar with the location of the home. He probably read about our home bust in the paper when we became famous. He came to us with his girlfriend.

She, dressed in a tight-fitting tank top with the inscription "It's a Bust," and he, a rather disheveled sort of person who claimed he was a Vietnam vet. Dylan, having served, decided to "give a vet a chance." I wondered about her shirt. He assured me it was just her lack of poor taste. Arrangements were made, and they gave us a substantial deposit and the first month's rent with the promise they would take good care of our property.

At first the rents were very timely. Then, suddenly, they ceased. Dylan finally called the tenants and they said there had been some sort of problem with the septic tank. For that reason they were withholding rent. By December Dylan decided he should fly back to the States and check it out. Arriving at the property, which was blanketed in two feet of snow, he realized he couldn't check out the septic tank without assistance. He hired a person with a backhoe to come in and dig up the property. Surprise! The tank was filled with hundreds of small plastic bags. Of course, the tenant claimed to know nothing about this. Clearly a raid had taken place at the house and they had flushed everything. This was verified by the state police.

To this day I don't know why we let them stay there, but stay they did. A year later, on a visit back to the States, I phoned my new friends, the state police, to see if all was OK. It wasn't. They wanted me to check out our house and see if there were any "suspicious containers, or dark curtains on the windows." They described what I should be looking for. Naively, I agreed. I reported back. Yep, they were making meth there. The house was raided, again. They, too, were thrown in jail. I was becoming way too familiar with what happens to folks who deal in drugs. We then rented our home out again. This was not a benefit of living overseas. Later in life I would recommend that clients not rent out their homes.

I did not know it at the time, but all of these crazy events I was challenged with would shape the person I would become. I was no longer the young girl who grew up on a farm in the country with no worldly experience. I was learning to expect the unexpected. I look back now and realize that these challenges began to change who I was to become and my role as a mother.

When we returned to Sao Paulo we settled into our individual routines. I returned to teaching in an all-day kindergarten class and was very involved with school activities. Life went on as normal as it could. Julina was six at the time and already was spending way too much time on the telephone. She was reading well and taking ballet lessons but was not terribly coordinated. She also had her Uncle Frank's charm of the gift of gab. Shanna was three and doing just about anything she could get away with. Dylan was working and taking off with Brazilian friends for weekends of hunting and fishing. His travel seemed incessant. He was always off to one place or another. I thought nothing of it at the time. I continued to sew and play my guitar in the evenings when he was gone once the kids were all in bed.

Mostly because of my pregnancy during this second tour, we limited our family travel to destinations within Brazil—Florianopolis, Blumenau, and Rio de Janeiro. Attending Carnival in Rio could have been the highlight of our tour if I had not been expecting at the time. The main parades didn't start until after midnight. The rocking and rolling of the three-story bleachers were rather unnerving in my condition. I was told it was an adventure not to be missed, but in my condition, I think I could have skipped that one.

Shortly after that little excursion, there was one other trip we made I will never forget. I guess Dylan thought if I could make it through Carnival in my condition, I could cope with anything. He wanted me to go on a fishing trip up the Amazon with him and friends. I was very apprehensive. He didn't tell me how far it was, but I was to find out. First, I flew to some unknown airport about four hours north on a harrowing flight through thunderous skies. He went by car with his friends and met me. Then we traveled fourteen hours by boat up the river, passing no signs of human life on this arduous trip. We finally arrived at some large rustic fishing camp, fortunately with netted tents as the mosquitoes were incessant. This was to be our base for the week. I was at least twenty hours away from the nearest doctor, and was so nervous I just wanted to cry. This would not have been my first choice as a vacation destination. I recall lying awake at night in the tent listening to the sounds of wildlife and the constant buzzing of mosquitoes wondering what in the hell I was doing there. I needed to go home for a rest. I decided then and there I would stay home until this baby was due. It was time to become more assertive.

We were living in Sao Paulo awaiting the birth. As we had already lived there, we were very familiar with the way of life, the language, the customs, and the traditions. Or so I thought. Having a baby in Brazil is a huge event. Well, it is everywhere, but the Brazilians adore children, and treat pregnant mothers with a reverence I had never experienced. My younger daughter Shanna was also born in Brazil some three years earlier. Apparently, I went about that all wrong. This time I would do things in the expected fashion, having on hand the required six plastic bags of matching baby outfits to hand over to the nurses at the hospital. I would also have at the ready a door decoration for the appropriate gender of our newborn. We were ready. But Dana was not.

This was 1982, before cell phones. International calls were very expensive. My baby was expected in mid-June. That didn't happen, nor the end of June. My mother kept calling me.

"No, Mom, I'm three weeks late!"

We had intended to take our annual home leave right after his birth to visit our families in the U.S., but clearly that was to be delayed. Exit visas having been obtained, we just sat and waited. I was finally scheduled for a Caesarean section July 2. Even in 1982, this was very common in Brazil.

July 2 was a momentous day in Brazil. Yes, because of the birth of my son, but also because Brazil was to play a World Cup soccer match in Spain against its archrival Argentina. I was all too familiar with the importance of that game to Brazilians. Because our home was near Morumbi Stadium, on any given weekend we could hear the roar of the fans when a goal was scored.

Upon arriving in the delivery room I noticed a large television placed right near the delivery table. My Brazilian doctor was not going to miss this very important game, I realized before I fell into an induced sleep. I recall thinking, "I really hope he is paying *me* some attention too!"

Brazil beat Argentina 3-1. The doctors and nurses were ecstatic. So was this mom. She finally had the baby boy she had been hoping for! Dana was named after his great-grandfather and weighed in at 3.55 kilos or 7.826 pounds, the largest of my three babies.

Birth accomplished, it was now time to ready our plans to head to the States. I was sent home from the hospital on July 7. My girls were thrilled to have a baby brother and hovered over him like a newly acquired doll. The next day my neighbor drove me to get Dana's picture taken for his passport and to register his birth. Five days after our arrival home from the hospital, we then took Dana to the US Consulate to get his passport. The following day we had to get his Brazilian passport. Two days later, we boarded our Varig flight to JFK. The flight attendants could not do enough for us. We had our hands full with a ten-day-old baby and two girls aged three and five, but their staff treated us like royalty. We were told numerous times what a beautiful family we had. Dana slept contently in a foldout basket next to me, oblivious to his first international flight.

We stayed for two weeks in New Jersey with my parents and then headed south for two weeks in Asheville, North Carolina, where Dylan's parents lived. Our school year in Brazil allowed us six weeks off in winter (our summer in the U.S.) and six weeks off in the summer. I had taught right up to Dana's birth but intended to take some leave upon our return to Brazil.

Instead, I returned to teach third grade shortly after our return to Sao Paulo because one of the teachers had to suddenly depart for her home in South Africa. We hired a wonderful gal named Judy who helped me take care of Dana from the time he was born. I was lucky to find her. When I asked her age she told me she was fifty-five. She was from Bahia and was very short and stout with dark skin and curly hair. I liked her immediately. I could sense she was a no-nonsense person. She replaced the previous nanny who for so many reasons was no longer with us.

Judy had come to us after working for a family who lived in the Interlagos part of the city. When I asked her why she wanted to leave, she relayed this story. The family she had worked for was quite comfortable and had several staff members plus a full-time driver. One day when only the wife and her staff were home, they were held up at gunpoint. Along with the others, Judy was held hostage while one of the assailants insisted that the wife write a check to cash for a large sum of money. They were held until the other went to the bank and successfully cashed the check. As the traffic in Sao Paulo is second to none, this took a few hours. They released everyone upon their return, but then stole the uninsured car of the family's driver. Crime was prevalent in Sao Paulo and one couldn't be too careful. The experience understandably terrified Judy so she immediately started making inquiries for other employment. I was only too happy to have her. I knew she would never open our gate to a stranger. That fact, combined with the large concrete wall topped with broken glass surrounding our house, a street guard, and our large newly acquired German shepherd Chips, helped to guarantee us some peace of mind. I was leaving my newborn son in these environs as I headed off to work each day.

Dana and Judy formed a special bond. He was her favorite. I think Julina, my oldest, just annoyed her as they were always bickering. Judy spoke no English, so of course we all conversed in Portuguese with her but English among ourselves. Having her in our midst every day, the children easily learned to converse in both languages. Perhaps because she was left-handed Dana also became left-handed. She used to hand him his fork with that hand. Years later, in college, Dana would write a paper about Judy when he was required to describe a person who had had a real impact on his life.

He somehow remembered the hours she would spend with him, singing songs or just chattering to him in Portuguese.

Our house was in order. Pictures were hung, an aquarium was set up for the kids, and projects were finished, including a large doll house I made for my girls. As TV wasn't a realistic pastime, we found other forms of entertainment. We read lots of books together and played games. Judy had her hands full with a newborn baby and trying to keep Chips from eating every plant in the garden. Shanna was learning to swim and Julina started to excel at reading. We fell into a pleasant routine, but then after just a few months we were informed that we would be leaving, again, soon. Dates were very uncertain. Just as we had gotten to somewhat of a regular schedule, it seemed we would be forced to reboot.

I was then enjoying teaching and training with Joyce Pickering, who would years later become president of the Board of Directors of the American Montessori Association. She and her husband Bob would later found and run Shelton School and Evaluation Center in Dallas, which was the world's largest private school for children with learning disabilities. Then, as she continues to do today, she ran a program teaching us to combine specialized reading instruction with the Montessori approach to learning. She had achieved a federal grant for this program for early childhood education. I realized at the time how fortunate I was to be working with such an incredible person. I did not realize at the time that the instruction I received would so benefit my newly born child.

By August 1982, plans were already in motion to return to the States. I was cleaning out closets, cupboards, and drawers in preparation for another sale. An ad was placed. The sale was to be between 9 a.m. and 5 p.m. Potential buyers started arriving at 7 a.m. I answered the phone no less than 200 times that day. At least 350 people came parading through the house. Not fun, but we managed to sell most things. Why? Because the company wanted us to keep our weight of the shipment down. I had three kids, including Dana who was only two months old, and we were running an enormous sale to save them money.

The girls didn't want to leave their dog Chips behind, but we didn't want to subject him to the six-week quarantine, so he found a new home with our neighbors. We sold our boat, packed up our shipment, and moved back to the Cadoro hotel for three weeks. Our plans got delayed as we were trying to obtain an exit visa for Judy so that she could accompany us home. The girls continued in school until we left. Continuity was important to me but extremely challenging. At last we finalized everything after attending many *despedida* parties, so common in our community. By then it was the beginning of November.

We arrived at JFK to very cold weather, a drastic change from our much warmer Brazil where it was currently summer. Our entourage consisted of me, Dylan, Judy, our three children, and twelve huge suitcases. The plan was to spend a few days in New York City and experience some of the culture we had missed for the past seven years. The trip from JFK required two large limos as all of us and all our belongings could not fit into one. Why so many suitcases? We would again, on this end, be waiting for our "shipment." Not furniture, just all our other worldly possessions. It was not to arrive for some six weeks.

Judy was there to assist with the children. This was her first time outside of Brazil. She had been overwhelmed by her first airplane flight, and now was standing in the middle of NYC in the freezing cold just gawking at her new surroundings. Sao Paulo was an immense city but its "skyscrapers" paled in comparison to what she was seeing now. "*Tao alto, tao alto!*" she kept repeating. So tall, so tall! Her next question to me was whether all the cars in the United States were yellow or black. For a moment I was confused. Then I realized, all she had seen at this point were yellow taxis and black limos. We were in New York. At that point it seemed like I had four children, not three, so we hurried indoors and finally got ourselves checked into the hotel, a monumental task. I was exhausted. Judy was in heaven. She ordered room service.

The rationale in bringing Judy back to the States with us was twofold. One, she had never had an experience like this in her life. Secondly, she could be of great assistance to me when we moved back to our "stone house" in Pennsylvania. Dylan was to take a position at the home office in New Jersey and the travel time was some two hours away. Not wanting to go house hunting immediately in New Jersey, we opted to stay in our home while he worked at the office and came home on weekends. I needed to get the girls in school. Julina was barely seven and Shanna was four. Dana was only five months and I had no family around to assist me, nor did I have a clue how to find a babysitter, especially in the middle of Berks County, where our nearest neighbor was almost a mile away. So Judy was with us. That also enabled me to complete writing my Montessori lesson books, which were required in the program I was still completing. This took hours and hours of writing, laborious step-by-step instruction for all the different lessons, math, phonics, science, etc. The person who invented White Out became my new best friend.

The environment we were in now, in Berks County, was the total antithesis of NYC. After just five days in the city, we drove out to our Pennsylvania home. We loved it for its charm and simplicity, just three bedrooms, timbered ceilings, and stone fireplaces. It had been converted from a Pennsylvania stone barn. We were situated on ten acres, quite a change from a suburban neighborhood in one of the largest cities in the world, on a property surrounded with walls. What we had there was near isolation. But we were home.

Dylan worked through January, commuting to Princeton or staying there and coming home on weekends. I was left to cope with the kids, but I had Judy to help. I tried my first attempts at skiing. My parents had since moved to North Carolina and were no longer in New Jersey, so visits to them were rare. At least I had some old friends from the area and was able to seek them out for company.

I thought we were settled in for the winter but by the end of January Dylan was offered a position at a new start-up company in Caracas, Venezuela. Did we want to take a trip down to check it out? I couldn't even comprehend yet another move but decided to listen. That's what wives do, right? We had a long discussion and agreed that, as Dylan was unhappy in his job, it seemed a viable idea. Having grown accustomed to, though not fond of, the packing and unpacking, we decided to give it some consideration. But first we were going to need to find a way to make the trip down to Caracas to check out the specifics about housing, schooling, and all other relevant information for yet another move. How were we to make this trip with three young children to consider? While I had Judy, who was perfectly capable of looking after the kids, there lay the problem of what she would do in an emergency. She didn't speak English. Leaving her with three small children in an environment she did not know was not a good option. Option two was to take all the kids. Not a good idea. Option three, which we settled upon, was to take Dana with us, and have the girls and Judy stay with family friends who lived in New Jersey. They had been like second parents to me while growing up and were only too glad to help. Thus it was that Dana went with us. He now was only five months old and had already traveled some 20,000 miles on a plane. By the time he was one, he would have flown twenty-one times.

After our visit to Venezuela, we decided to make the move. Dylan went ahead to start his new job while I remained temporarily in Pennsylvania with Judy and the kids. In preparation, we then had to make plans to rent out our home again. We spent Christmas in Asheville, North Carolina, with Dylan's parents where we were joined by his sister and her family from California. Dylan made a video of our family that year. I had taught the girls and their cousins Christmas songs and made Santa hats for them so they could perform for the family. (This video has become the family "go to" for me and my kids every Christmas since then. It has been recorded and rerecorded. Every time we see it we howl. The first question each Christmas is, "When are we going to watch Christmas '82?") The most nostalgic thing for me in watching it is realizing that was the first time we had been together with the whole family at Christmas since my children had been born.

After the holidays, we still couldn't move yet as plans had not been finalized. I had to go back to Pennsylvania with Judy and the girls to wait on our Venezuelan visas. Also, the lawyers were having a difficult time getting Judy a work permit. We had decided to ask her if she wanted to move to Caracas with us or return to Brazil. She wanted to stay with us. She was very attached to Dana.

The delay also was that Dylan was in Colombia at that time working on some joint venture with his boss. He was then to be in Caracas the following week, preparing for a meeting the week after in New Jersey. Then he had to go to Mexico for three days, meaning he wouldn't return to Pennsylvania until the February 19. Nothing seemed to be moving along smoothly. That was not a fun winter. It had turned very cold and snowy, so getting the girls out to school became a challenge. But the girls were doing well. Julina had gotten all A's and B's on her report card, and Shanna had gotten all S's except for one. Apparently, she failed at "knows address and phone number." This was not unexpected. Even I was confused at that point.

Fortunately for Dana, none of this affected him, except for the fact his dad was seldom around. He got his first tooth at seven months, on the bottom, and I took him for his checkups. He was average weight and height and we made fresh baby food for him every day. He spent a lot of time bouncing in his "kangaroo," that thing we used to hang from door frames. It was his favorite. He was happy because I was around and Judy and his sisters as well. Judy was getting used to the snow. The first time she saw it she ran outside barefoot and stuck out her tongue to catch snowflakes. In her fifty-five years she said that was one of the most exciting things she ever experienced. I told her to enjoy the snow. Where we were moving next, there would be none.

CHAPTER 6

1983 CARACAS

WE FINALLY RECEIVED the green light to move at the end of February. Suitcases were packed, again. And we rented out our home, again. This time we headed to the Tomanaco Hotel in Caracas which in its day was lovely. Today as I watch the news I am so distraught over what has become of the country, but in 1983 it was considered safe, though it did have its share of crime. Again, I went in search of a house to rent. It took forever. We had arrived around Carnival time and no one was working. After two weeks of searching I found the perfect place in Chuao. It wasn't near the school, but they had buses for the girls. It was in a great neighborhood near a park where Judy could go with Dana.

Our stay in the hotel lasted almost two months as we waited for our shipment. This time I insisted we were taking all our things. I was sick of half of our belongings being in storage. While unpacking, I noticed the bill of lading and realized we had moved 28,000 pounds. This was not surprising. Every time we moved we accumulated more, even though we had had many sales. For this reason, it took me weeks to unpack. We finally moved in on March 25. Two days afterward, I woke up to find a huge cockroach on my arm. I raced to the shower.

One jumped on me there, where I screamed loudly. We then had to move out so the house could be fumigated. So much for our perfect house. Living overseas again was proving to test my patience.

We moved back in, bought another boat, and started living life. I loved it there, especially the climate. It was in the 80s every day, with clear skies and the occasional rain shower. The air was cleaner and fresher. I started tutoring students in English as it was midyear in the school term. The best part, though, was that our friends whom we previously had become very close to in Brazil had made the same move. We were fortunate to have a readymade extended family. This time Sarah and I finally found the right wardrobe for me. I had my hair cut short and started on a Jane Fonda routine which did its magic on transforming my body. We changed our evenings, though. This time when the "boys" were away, we would go out together and explore the many great restaurants of Caracas. I was starting to be a much more independent Mom.

We continued our camping trips together and headed toward the beaches of Venezuela. Then we got it in our heads to make a trip through the interior of Venezuela to Brazil some twenty hours away. We planned to travel with four other families. By necessity we had to carry our own food, gas, tents, generators, lights, and enough drinks for eighteen people to last for ten days. Even though we had a well-planned trip we experienced some pretty wild and harrowing moments. On virtually nonexistent roads, three cars in our caravan managed to get hung up on rocks. It took a lot of manpower to extricate them. To further test our patience, we were stopped at many checkpoints with guns pointed at us. Then there was the wildlife, lots of it and not all friendly. There were six young children on this trip and they were great sports about everything, including bathing under waterfalls, our only option. Dana was only one at the time and while he couldn't talk much, he never complained and loved his waterfall baths. I don't camp anymore. Camping to me now is slow room service. While it was great fun, I think that particular trip cured me for life.

While some of our family and friends back in the States thought we were leading rather glamorous lives, I can assure you that Venezuela, even then, had its challenges. Our biggest challenge was to keep a car. We kept our boat at a marina about four hours south of Caracas in Puerto la Cruz. The islands off the coast were magnificent so it was worth the drive. One weekend we took the girls down. Dana was still a bit small to manage in a boat all day. Our marina was guarded with a gate and two guards. We arrived, unloaded, and went out fishing and swimming for the day. Upon our return we couldn't find our car. It had been stolen. The girls were terribly upset because their Barbies were in it. I was upset because we were dressed for boating and all our other clothes were in the car. Dylan was upset because we didn't have a car to get home. We spent the night at the nearby hotel and called for a taxi in the morning to take us to the local airport. The airline said we couldn't travel as we didn't have our ID cards or passports with us. Of course, we didn't. We had been robbed of our car and hadn't planned on flying. Much discussion and yelling went on for about an hour. They finally let us board. I think we mentioned the US Consulate.

We arrived back in Caracas by plane and were now officially carless. Since our friends Sarah and Jim were traveling, we asked to borrow theirs for the week. Jim was with the same company as Dylan, so this seemed reasonable. We went to some friends' home that Saturday evening for a party and parked on the street as did many others. When we left the party, there was no car to be found. It, too, had been stolen. Julina, then seven, suggested we just buy some extras. The company gave us a hard time for "losing" cars. Then they said they wouldn't insure them. Yeah, right. It was two months before we got them replaced. SUVs were apparently highly sought commodities for running drugs through the interior into Columbia. Ah, Venezuela! It would be an understatement to say I was rarely relaxed.

By May, Dana was running around in his walker. He was also slyly getting into everything. This was adding to my stress as we had many levels, many stairs, and no baby gates. I tried tying up tennis nets. The carpenter was two months late in showing up to make some gates. Judy and I had our hands full trying to keep tabs on him. He grew four more teeth and would put anything in his mouth he could get his hands on.

Dylan was constantly traveling for business. He logged over 100,000 miles that year. He told me the economy in Latin America was not doing great and these trips were necessary. By August he managed to hit San Francisco, Chicago, New Jersey, and Brazil in a period of just two weeks. After that trip he said that it would probably be eighteen months before the company would resolve their Latin American holdings. Once that happened, he announced, we would most likely be sent somewhere else. This was not news I wanted to hear. I did not even want to think about moving. I had just hung the last of the pictures, organized the house, and had just begun to prepare my classroom for the upcoming school year. I was now to teach at the international school, Campo Alegre. I was in the middle of working on my doctoral degree when we left Brazil, as I was able to take courses through Virginia Tech. I wanted to get my certification in administration. A move was not something I wanted to consider but it was not put to a vote.

We had planned a visit back to the States in July for Dana's first birthday. At the last minute that plan changed as Dylan had to travel again to another meeting in the States. It was so frustrating because nothing it seemed ever went according to plan. As Judy was off to visit her family in Brazil for a month, I revised our trip. Better to be away while she wasn't around to help.

With some trepidation, I headed off alone with the kids to the States. It's no fun traveling with three children alone on a long international flight, but I was getting used to managing on my own. We flew up to Asheville to Dylan's parents for the week. After a lot of deliberation I decided to drive up to Virginia Tech in Blacksburg for a few weeks to try and finish up my degree. Dylan's's parents offered to watch the kids. I was thrilled, as were the kids. The three of them were always delighted to stay with their grandparents. After driving away from their home, I experienced freedom I hadn't felt in a long time. No kids, no job, no demands, no planning or moving. I threw myself into my studies for three weeks and then returned to Asheville to retrieve my children. As a bonus, they had somehow managed to potty-train Dana while I was away.

At the end of our winter break (summer in the US), we returned to our routine of school, work, and spending time down on our boat. Dana was now learning to fish off the boat with his dad. While we had been away, Judy had been to visit her family in Bahia, in the north of Brazil. Upon her return, we heard her conversing on the phone with someone. We could tell she was extremely distraught. We heard her telling whoever she was speaking to that she wanted her brother dead. She was literally hiring someone to do this for her. Dylan took the phone and tried to calm her, asking her what was going on. Sobbing, she told us that most of the money that we had been paying her for the past several years she had sent to her mother in Bahia. Apparently, her brother had intercepted this money and taken it for himself. She was in the process of hiring someone to kill him. Guns for hire were not unusual in Brazil, but we did put a stop to that one.

In spite of the challenges, our time in Venezuela was rewarding for me. By the time I returned from our home leave, I was able to return to teaching and also take the position as assistant principal at the school. Despite the many, many moves I felt I was at least keeping my professional life on track. This was not easy as every time I became settled into a school it was time to leave and start over. Fortunately, many of our friends were in the same situation and it made it easy to transition. We made new friends at a nearby club where Dylan and I would play golf or tennis nearly every weekend when we weren't on our boat. Our girls were thriving in their school and activities. Julina began taking gymnastics lessons, which would carry her later into competition and some coaching. As Dana was too young yet for preschool, he spent his days with Judy perfecting his Portuguese. She was such a loving and caring individual. Caracas holds great memories for me because we were able to do things as a family when Dylan was around and not traveling.

In 1984, just as our lives had settled into a comfortable routine, we got the word. We would be moving back to the States. Because the company headquarters were in New Jersey we assumed that's where we would be going. We were told the company wanted us to move to California. I could deal with Thailand, Brazil, and Venezuela but really had my doubts about a move to California. I hadn't heard good things about the school system. I also did not want to again be so far from our families who were all on the East Coast. We decided to make a trip out there to check it out and stayed about a week. I wasn't impressed and emphatically said I really didn't want to relocate there. So, New Jersey was to become our next destination. I had been too far from my family for too long.

Once our destination had been established, my next step was to try and find a teaching position. I wanted to get a head start on this as I knew that by midyear most school systems were planning for the next. I immediately wrote some letters to see what might be available. I had met a friend at Virginia Tech the prior summer who I knew could help, as her husband was a superintendent in a neighboring state and had lots of connections. So I called Sheila and *voila*, I had some interviews. That accomplished, I flew up to New Jersey for a week. I was greatly interested in the school district where I assumed we would be moving as the company headquarters were located there. The superintendent there was most accommodating. After the interview he took me to lunch and showed me around the charming suburban town, pointing out neighborhoods that we should consider. Feeling great about this, I went back to the hotel to unwind. After a relaxing dinner I was having a drink at the bar and guess who walked in? After a few minutes of conversation, it suddenly dawned on me why he was there. I calmly told the superintendent that I was not interested and if that is how prospective candidates were guaranteed a position, he could be assured I would not be joining his team. "Me Too" hadn't even been thought of then. As it turned out, we did not move to that town, because the following week the company announced its plans to move its headquarters to a different part of New Jersey known as Murray Hill. The superintendent of the district I eventually ended up working for was no prize either. It was no wonder that I became disillusioned with public education.

During the time I was traveling, Dylan took the responsibility for the packing of the house. This was the first time it didn't fall on me to do it and I felt I was given an unexpected holiday. I returned to Caracas and an upside-down household at the end of the process. After packing up all our worldly possessions, and selling the boat and the cars, we headed to the hotel. This was going to be a difficult move for so many reasons. There was no way we could take Judy with us as we couldn't get her a work visa. She was to be separated from Dana for the first time. Dana was almost three at the time. We arranged for Judy to go and work for our good friends, Sarah and Jim. All I can say was that it was a very tearful goodbye at the airport.

Upon arrival back to the States we were greeted by a large snowstorm. Off to the mall to buy snowsuits to outfit my three freezing children. Next it was house hunting time. We still owned our stone house in Pennsylvania, but we still had tenants in it, decent ones this time. We needed a short-term rental, impossible to find as we weren't sure where we wanted to eventually buy. We finally found one, and only one, furnished, in Summit. Our shipment, of course, was still in transit.

After the Christmas season I enrolled the girls in school. Dana stayed home with me. This was the first time I had no help since my oldest was born. Because I now had no babysitter I had to take Dana with me on one of my job interviews. I landed a job as a substitute teacher in the school system. The only glitch was that they never knew until that morning if they needed someone. I would awake to a 6 a.m. call, dress the kids for school, drop Dana at the preschool in the next town, and then show up for work. I did this only because

I knew I had a better shot of obtaining a full-time position if I first subbed in the system.

The hours spent not teaching were spent looking for a home to purchase. We had already decided to sell our Pennsylvania home as geographically it made no sense. We did find a buyer and set out to find the perfect home in Summit. Not easy. The prices were high, and we had three kids and a lot of stuff. While looking at more than sixty homes in and around the area it occurred to me that maybe I should get my real estate license. This area was much easier to navigate than any place we had ever lived and I knew I could help people with their whole moving process. I had just done it sixteen times in the past fourteen years. That decision made, I began my real estate courses that winter. The plan was to do it only part time.

We found a home and moved, again, after just six months in the rental house. I didn't love the house, but it fit our needs offering lots of space and a good neighborhood. After a few months, though, I realized the girls and Dana were never going to be able to walk to school because it would entail crossing a very busy main road. My dream at this point was for them to be able to walk everywhere, school, town, or friends' houses. That's when kids could do that. We certainly never had that in Brazil or Venezuela, just gates, walls and fences. The hunt was now on again for a better location. I now had my real estate license and so began the search. The home we were currently in was not going to sell without some sweat equity, so the process began of stripping wallpaper, repainting, and making it more appealing. The home sold in seven days and we were able to jump on one we found very near the town and school. We won it, too, in another bidding war. So there was yet another move to make. At the time, we considered it to be our last one. We loved the house, the location, and the neighborhood and saw no reason to ever have to leave it.

It was during this time that I was offered a full-time a position teaching sixth grade. A position had opened because a teacher had gone on maternity leave. I juggled my life, getting the girls ready for school, dropping Dana at preschool every day, and picking him up afterward. I thought I did a pretty good job of managing without help. At the conclusion of the school year, I was told that I would have the position for the following year, as well. They lied. I subsequently found out, at a party at my house for the staff, that another teacher had in fact been hired. I became aggravated and frustrated when I later found out that the person who was offered the full-time position had only two years of teaching experience versus my thirteen. I also had a master's degree plus thirty hours towards my doctoral degree. I was simply too expensive. Yielding to my frustration, I decided to take some time off and pursue real estate part-time instead. That was to be the last time I would teach. I was so disillusioned by the school administration I decided my time was better spent trying to take care of my own kids. I had no idea at the time that by starting a career in real estate I would, instead, be forced to spend so much time away from them.

CHAPTER 7

1987-1993 THE "ALL-AMERICAN FAMILY"

THE FIRST FOUR or five years we lived in Summit were rather typical of many American families. Compared to all that had preceded I felt we were finally on the track of normalcy. Dylan worked in nearby Murray Hill, the kids had their school within walking distance, and I worked full time in real estate. The kids settled into a routine life of school, activities, and sports. I felt blessed that we had returned to the States and were going to lead a normal life for a change.

Dana was never a problem child. He was the cutest towhead on the block with big brown eyes. His affectionate nature was endearing. No matter how many times I kissed him goodbye before heading out to an appointment, he would always race to the door, stand there, and wave. I wasn't allowed to leave until he saw me wave back. He also was outgoing and full of energy. More than anything, he just wanted to make friends and hit and kick balls around. When he was growing up, the new computer Game Boys were all the rage. He had limited interest in those or anything else that kept him indoors. Just let him out and he was down our street in a flash seeking out friends who wanted to play.

Dana was the smallest in his class when he started kindergarten at his new school. He got teased a lot. He was so friendly and wanted everyone to like him but got excluded from many birthday parties and the like because of his size. But he was resilient, and despite this he managed to make friends. One he became very close to, Sean, lived in the neighborhood and the two of them were constantly together. When Sean's family moved away years later, Dana was devastated.

I was advised more than once by his teachers at the elementary school that Dana had a short attention span. I was very aware of this and not unversed in how it affects the learning process. I had been teaching school for over fifteen years and had many students who were affected by some sort of learning disability. I had been trained by an excellent mentor, Joyce Pickering, who was my principal in Escola Graduada in Sao Paulo. During my teaching there, I never suggested to any parents that they should explore the possibility of the then-popular drug Ritalin. This was a well-known drug which professed to improve a student's focus and allow the child to become less distracted by outside factors. I remember very well one third grader I taught who could never remember to take books home or do homework assignments. We devised a system that we followed every single day. I made sure he left with his "notebook" to be read and signed by his parents as to what his assignments were and what he needed to return. It was very effective. I knew with proper managing and parental cooperation, we as a team could control for the most part even the most disorganized child. So when it was recommended to me that Dana be prescribed this drug, it was a firm no.

Dana had a condition known as Attention Deficit Hyperactivity Disorder (ADHD). This condition usually starts in childhood and can persist into adulthood. Treatment can help, but this condition can't be cured. It can last for years or last a lifetime. I had been trained to spot the signs and they were all there. The symptoms include limited attention, lack of impulse control, and hyperactivity. I explained this to his teachers, more than one, year after year, and told them that this was the core of his inability to focus and that together we would manage it. And we did. Dana got good grades, and I always was on top of what was expected of him and somehow he managed to get it done. I always found that in structuring a schedule, he was much more organized. Sports became a key factor in helping him to maintain focus.

Dana was happiest when he was on the move. He started tee ball in first grade and then moved on to baseball and soccer. Biking was one of his favorite activities. He would bike all over town with his friends, disappearing for hours. And he loved to run. Towards the end of elementary school, he participated in a one-mile race. When the girls and I arrived to cheer him on, we noticed he was so far ahead of everyone else it didn't seem like he was running the same race. When the trophies were handed out he tearfully came up to me and told me they didn't have one for him. Of course I jumped in to see why. It seemed they had mistakenly entered his name on the girl's roster. At this point it occurred to me that potential future problems could arise. It was like having a boy named Sue, to quote Johnny Cash. He had been named after his great-grandfather and I guess hadn't realized the popularity of this as a girl's name.

Dana wanted in the worst way to be a Cub Scout, so he joined the local pack. He marched proudly down the main street of town in the Memorial Day parade with his new friends. He was grinning ear to ear as we cheered him when he walked by. Dylan of course took pictures.

Dana also loved playing the trumpet. He started playing in elementary school and played in the school band. He continued when he got to middle school and we all had to endure his long practice rehearsals in the house.

We were a close-knit family in the 1980s. During the kids' winter breaks our family would ski together. This wasn't an easy feat with three children. Just getting them on the ski lift was a challenge. We made our way to New York, Vermont, Pennsylvania, and one winter to Colorado. The kids all loved the sport and Dana had learned at the young age of three. In the summers we would often take our boat and rent a house at the Jersey Shore.

By the late '80s our destination changed to Hilton Head, South Carolina, and we would drive there with our boat in tow and all three kids packed into our Suburban. We would put in at the marina in Harbor Town, laughing that we were the smallest boat there. It didn't matter. We'd drag the kids around for hours tubing or water skiing off the coast of Daufuskie Island. Our weekends at home were spent hanging out at our pool or boating off the Jersey Shore. Unfortunately, the boat day trips took on a life of their own as we would, upon Dylan's insistence, spend hours cleaning it before heading home. The kids gradually became less enamored with these outings and found excuses not to go. I was working more and on weekends and it became harder for me to get away.

Each summer we sent the kids to camp for two weeks. Because they had spent so many years deprived of fresh outdoor living, I was determined that they have these opportunities once we moved back to the States. Their camps were in the North Carolina Smoky Mountains. The location was perfect as I could put them on the plane and Dylan's parents would meet them in Asheville and take them over to camp. Ruth and John loved doing this because it gave them more time with their grandkids. They visited them at camp on the weekends when visitors were encouraged, and spoiled them with pizza and ice cream. These summers were special for both the kids and them. After camp sessions, the kids would return to their grandparents' home and spend a week. Dana would ride around for hours in his granddad's golf cart or help him out in his huge garden. They developed a closeness that would endure forever.

During the school year, as it falls to most mothers, I was in charge of the kids' activities, sports, parent/teacher conferences, and all things kids related. Today as I watch my daughters' families I realize how much has changed. The daddies now get very involved in every aspect of their child's life, school, sports, eating habits, and every other conceivable thing that could influence their lives. Privately I wished this could have happened in my children's lives, but it wasn't to be. As I was working many more hours at my job, it became a real challenge. I had to hire someone to help with the kids' meals because I was rarely home in the early evenings due to work. Then it was supervising homework and organizing for the next day. Mostly it became a challenge to stay positive in my marriage. From the outside it probably looked perfect. It wasn't.

Dylan was less than enthusiastic about our town. He found the people pompous and would make derogatory remarks about his co-workers. He started spending an inordinate amount of time in our garage working on the boat or some other project that didn't involve being around people. His lack of involvement precipitated many arguments and was most likely the reason I realized I was living the life of a single parent, even while married. Personally, I loved where we lived. I loved having no privacy walls, not having to cope with stolen cars, or worrying about revolutions. Mostly I loved the freedom the children had, which they didn't have before.

To try and remain social, I had arranged one night for us to go out to dinner with another couple who had also lived in Brazil. Julina was sixteen by this time and well able to look after herself and her two siblings. I fed them before we left and told them to make sure after some TV that they locked the house and got to bed early. When we arrived home we realized that we did not have the key to the front door. The back was locked as well. We checked our "secret rock" where a key was hidden. Apparently, it wasn't so secret because it appeared that one of the kids had taken it. We rang the bell numerous times but couldn't seem to wake the kids. Dylan went to the glove compartment of the car and announced to me and our friends, "Stand back!"

"What are you doing?" I cried when I saw he had a gun in his hand.

"Opening the door," he said calmly. And then he blasted a bullet at the lock. I just stood there. Who was this man?

After that incident, I don't remember being asked to dine out with friends again. Things were spiraling downhill. Dylan's involvement with our kids became less and less. It seemed it was always up to me to take them to their sporting events and coordinate activities for them. Gradually we stopped doing things as a family as often. Our last trip together to Hilton Head was 1990. We had stopped on the way to visit my mother, who was very sick in the hospital at Duke University. She had been diagnosed with leukemia on May 30. I didn't recognize her then in July. She died on my birthday in August. It was a very difficult time for me and I felt her loss immensely. I realized then how many years we had spent apart with all of our international moves and was saddened by how much time we had missed together.

When Dylan lost his job in 1991 and was home for many months, things got worse. As I was still working crazy hours, I expected more from him and was disappointed when that didn't happen. It fell to me to then be responsible for the mortgage as well. These combined factors do not for a healthy marriage make. He eventually got a job in New York and then was commuting every day to the city, not getting home until 7:30 or 8 each evening. We rarely had dinner as a family because the kids were too hungry to wait. Our lives were unraveling. It was evident Dylan did not like his job in the city, nor was he fond of "suburban living" and everything it represented. I began to wonder if the glue that had held us together was all the moving we had done. We started mediation in 1992 and got divorced in 1993. Dana was eleven years old.

CHAPTER 8

1993

THE YEAR 1993 stands in my mind as one of the turning points in our lives. I made some good choices, but I also made some bad ones. Prior to our divorce I had struck up a relationship with a person I'll call David. I had met him through real estate as a client and we started seeing one another. This was not a secret from my soon-to-be ex. We had already agreed to divorce and things were being finalized and possessions equally distributed. Dylan stayed in the house during this time, though that wasn't my first choice. The kids were all aware of what was transpiring.

My girls, who were seventeen and fourteen at the time, were not surprised and expressed to me when I told them we were divorcing, "It's about time, Mom. You two do nothing but fight." Upon hearing that, I realized they knew I was making the right decision. In hindsight though, I probably should have waited a while before introducing them to David. Although the marriage wasn't right, I shouldn't have jumped into a new relationship.

I have to believe my judgment was clouded. Having had to be responsible for pretty much everything regarding the household and the kids' lives for the past couple of years, I was looking to somehow improve my life. I was looking for someone to share good times with again. I wanted to laugh, to dance, go out to dinner, and be happy. This all happened with David at first. We were inseparable. I wanted to be with him, and he with me. A few months later he gave up his apartment and moved into my house. With his untrained dog.

Originally David was the perfect boyfriend. We went to dinner every week, went to movies, and I introduced him to my friends who were all so happy to see me smile again. He volunteered to be a soccer coach in Dana's league and was assigned to his team. That first year for spring break, we decided to take Julina, Shanna, Dana, and a friend each to Florida. This was all quite new to Dana, who was not sure how to treat David. I have to believe it was very confusing to him. The week went well, though I don't ever remember seeing kids trash a room like they did. Perhaps it was a little rebellion?

After a few months my girls came to like David less and less. They complained he treated the house like it was his and not theirs. Their method of acting out came one evening when David and I went to dinner. While we awaited our meal, the waiter approached our table and said there was a phone call for me. I had always told the kids our destination so if they needed to reach me they could. No cell phones then. I took the call and realized I was talking to the town police. I was to come home immediately. Of course, I responded that I would. David was angry. They had ruined our night out.

Upon arriving home, I was informed the girls had "hosted" an underage drinking party. That isn't actually what happened. There was a party, and yes, it was at my house. Even before cell phones kids knew who was going to be home and who wasn't. So my house was targeted that night. All the kids phoned one another and *voila*, there were some thirty kids there and they had been busted. I was not happy. All the parents were called to come and get their kids and of course daggers were shot my way like it was my fault this happened. It was pretty much, *What did you expect? She's divorced with three kids.*

I knew when I got divorced things weren't going to be easy, but I hadn't expected this. The girls were of course sorry and said it wasn't their fault. They kept trying to tell everyone to go home. They hadn't invited anyone. They had never done anything like this before. Dana was home at the time. According to the girls he hid under his bed when the police came. He was a little traumatized. He kept asking what I was going to do to the girls. So life wasn't quite what I expected it to be. But I was sure we could all work it out.

While all this was going on, Dylan was living nearby in the adjacent town. After our divorce we decided he should be local so that the kids could continue to see him weekends. Dana and the girls went to his condo often to visit but complained he hadn't really unpacked yet. It didn't feel like home at all to them. With a stranger in our house, I don't think our home felt like home either.

Six months after Dylan moved into his condo, his new company decided to send him to Brazil. This time he was to be sent to the interior to Minas Gerais. While today it ranks as the second most populous state in Brazil, at that time it was very underdeveloped. It didn't have an expat population, American schools, or anything the least bit enticing as a place to live. At the time I remember feeling euphoric that this was a move I didn't have to make. As our relationship was strained, I wasn't unhappy he was leaving the country. I had no idea if his moving down there would have any impact on our children's lives, but it didn't make a difference what I thought. That's where he chose to go. Who knows? Maybe it didn't make any difference. Dylan accepted the position and returned to Brazil. That summer Dana flew down to spend it with his dad. He became quite proficient in Portuguese as no English was spoken there. I was relieved he was away from my home because things were falling apart.

Before Dana left for the summer, unsettling incidents kept occurring which affected my entire household. David's dog became the first problem. He had not trained it. I should have seen this as the first sign of irresponsibility. We started having many arguments about the dog peeing in my house and whose fault it was. I finally put a wall up with plywood in the kitchen to contain it. Neither David nor the dog was a fan of this solution. The second problem was how he spent money, money he didn't have. For some reason, in the beginning, call it love, call it stupidity, I had helped him buy a car. He didn't have good credit, so I decided to help him. I also gave him my second AmEx card. Don't ask me why. Later self-examination would reveal all the stupid decisions I made regarding this relationship. I was told by a then-friend that I was becoming "an enabler." I should have listened to her.

I was also to learn that David had a temper. One evening I questioned him about something and he got irrationally angry. I threw a dish of coins across the room. For some reason he became unglued, perhaps former family history? Who knows? But at that point he physically grabbed me. My girls heard the commotion, came running in yelling at him, and called the police. The police arrived and what did I do? I told them it was just a misunderstanding and that everything was fine. Actually, everything clearly wasn't fine, but I wanted it to be. This now was the second time in less than a year the police had cause to come to my home. Not a good sign. Dana wasn't home at the time, but you can be sure the girls told him about it.

Despite my apprehensions, I let him stay, also a bad decision. But as time went on I also began to mistrust him, for many valid reasons. In the late spring we had planned a trip to Washington, D.C., to take Dana and his friend Sean for a long weekend. David told me at the last minute he had to work the day we were leaving but he would take the train and meet me down there. On the first day, I took Dana and his friend to the many museums along the National Mall, but my heart wasn't in it. I hadn't heard from David and wondered why. I gave him the benefit of the doubt, though, and figured he'd be arriving the next morning. The following morning I phoned my daughter to see if he had left the house yet for the train. He hadn't. He was sleeping. I told her to go wake him up. I was livid. We had promised to do this trip with Dana together. He assured me that he wanted to come but just couldn't because of some work obligations. When I finally arrived home two days later, I discovered that his "work obligations" had included a movie and dinner for two at a nearby restaurant. How? I went through his pockets and found receipts.

And thus, I became a proficient but very disillusioned sleuth. I soon discovered charges to my AmEx card for hotels I hadn't slept in and dinners I hadn't been invited to. This evidence, compounded with the fact he was missing many soccer games he was committed to and missing commitments he had made to Dana, opened my eyes to what I had gotten myself into. Moreover, I had now subjected my kids to this lying, cheating person living in my house. The worst part of this time is that I knew I was so involved in my feelings for him and being hurt, that I wasn't as focused on my kids as I needed to be. My friends, having heard all my tales of woe about this deteriorating relationship, encouraged me to get rid of him. That decision became an easy choice.

One Friday we decided the two of us would stay in for dinner instead of dining out. My daughters were out with friends for the evening and Dana was away in Brazil visiting his dad. I prepared the dinner and waited for David to make his arrival. It became later and later. I became more and more agitated. Dinner was getting ruined. Where the hell was he? His train should have arrived hours ago. By about 9:30 I had about had it. I called my good friend Dotty who was in the know about how this once "wonderful" relationship had gone south. I tearfully told her what was going on. She calmly suggested I pack some of his things, put them at the back door, and tie the dog to the fence outside. After a great deal of discussion, I admitted she was right and agreed to do what she suggested.

At 10:15 I heard a banging on the back door and David yelling to let him in. I had locked him out. He didn't have a key and I had removed the one from our "hidden rock." He was irate, screaming that I had to let him in. I didn't answer. I then heard him yell that he was going to go and get the police. *Great!* I thought, *Let him.* A few minutes later he did arrive with an officer who had been conveniently up the street checking out something at the nearby private school. When I opened the door to him standing there with David, I just smiled. The policeman was Tony, whom I knew because I had just done a market analysis for him on his home. Tony had no idea it was my home he was being called to. As I opened the door, he asked me what was going on.

"Tony, this *person* (not what I really said) has been living in my house with me and my three kids. I have been making his meals, doing his laundry, walking his dog and cleaning up after him and the pooch, who by the way has been crapping all over my house. He has been out with other women, cheating, lying and tonight God knows where he has been. He clearly has other interests than me. He is not welcome here anymore."

David tried to tell him he had been at Barnes & Noble, in the next town, seven miles away. He claimed he had walked from there. He wasn't even a good liar. Tony at this point had heard enough, looked at David, and said, "You, go wait in my car." Then he turned to me and said, "Linda, can you make me some coffee? Let's talk about this." I felt like a weight had been lifted from my shoulders. Tony became my hero. For years afterward when I saw him in town, I called him "Tony, My Hero."

That night, after him asking me what to do with David, I told him to take him to his other girlfriend's. You see, I knew he had one. I had been doing some sleuthing. The prior week I had found out she had a condo in Summit and that's where he had been spending some time. We won't go into my sleuthing techniques, but damn I became good. Having successfully ousted him from the household (possessions would follow later), the next day I gleefully took the car I had bought for David to the local dealer. I told him I only wanted to sell it for whatever was left on the balance on the payments for the car. The prior payments had been made by David. He would not recoup a cent. He now had no place to live unless someone took him in, and no means of transportation. For the first time in two years, I felt good. Shame on me, but I needed to move on.

The importance of that evening was very impactful. I realized it was now the third time the police had been to my home. That was it. I was done. I was finished with having men disrupt our lives by their selfish acts and stupidity. My distrust in men was growing by leaps and bounds. I decided that as a mother, I would never put myself or my children in that situation again. I needed to pay more attention. I was going to be the best mom ever. I had three children who were dependent on me. Well, my daughters weren't exactly children, but their lives were going to be impacted if I didn't make some changes.

It was shortly after this little scenario played out that I received a very distressful phone call from my eldest, who was now in her second year at Colgate University. She said her dad had told her that he really didn't want her to continue at Colgate. He wanted her to go somewhere less expensive. He had already expressed the same thoughts to me saying that Julina wasn't the smart one. Shanna was, and the cost of sending Julina to Colgate was ridiculous. I, as a result, became extremely annoyed at Dylan. He was not exactly being the supportive father I had expected. My confidence in men was plummeting by the minute. I told Julina that no matter what, I would make sure she would stay in that school. I didn't care how many houses I had to sell but I would make it happen. She didn't speak with her dad for years. I didn't either.

Once David was removed from our household, life went on in a much calmer fashion. Dana was now in his last year of middle school and playing a lot of ice hockey. He was playing on the Beacon Hill team and a lot of the games were away. Shanna wasn't old enough to drive so I was constantly trying to arrange carpools for his games and practices to fit my work schedule. The games were mostly early Sunday mornings. One Sunday in January we awoke to over a foot of snow. I groaned when I saw what had to happen. The whole driveway was going to need to be shoveled before I could get out. Again, I had to phone a friend to get a ride for Dana. The game was in Princeton, a good hour away. I shoveled the driveway as best I could to get out and took off. I made good time, too good, according to the police officer who gave me a speeding ticket. Apparently, he didn't have kids who played hockey. He was immune to my tale of woe and single parenting. Fortunately, I did make the game and then all the families went to breakfast afterward. I kept looking at my watch. I still needed to drive home, shower, dress, and prepare for an open house that afternoon. I was already exhausted. Hockey parents are always exhausted. It takes over your life.

I will admit that I was juggling a lot of balls at the time. In addition to working every day, I worked nearly every weekend, taking clients out or holding open houses. I came to realize I could not do this all alone, so finally hired a person to help out in the afternoons. She would be there when Dana and Shanna came home from school. She often would feed them their dinner as I had many evening appointments doing real estate. I knew I had to work even harder if I were to make a go of this on my own. I really had only my brothers to talk to. My mom was gone and I didn't want my dad to worry about me. I was determined to be strong and independent. When I did speak with him, I always assured him everything was fine.

One evening my brother Jim called me to check in and see how I was faring. I was on the kitchen phone upstairs and apparently the door to the basement was ajar. I was telling Jim about the former indiscretion by my now ex-husband. I had never mentioned this to anyone in the family and they were all in the dark about the events that had taken place so many years ago. It was a fact that I had kept a secret but clearly hadn't forgotten. Now that we were divorced it no longer mattered who knew. I then laughed and told him that somewhere there was a fourteen-year-old kid who didn't even know his or her father. Shanna, unbeknownst to me, was down in the basement and happened to hear the end of this conversation. After the call she came up to me completely bewildered and asked if she was adopted. I assured her she was not and decided then I had to share the story with my girls. Dana was not around for this. Had he been, I don't know if I would have told him. He was only eleven.

Because of our divorce agreement, I was to sell the family home at the end of Dana's middle school years. Why I agreed to this I have no idea. This was the home I thought we would be in forever, while the kids were growing up. I really didn't want to sell and move yet again. But the house was rather large and with Shanna soon to go off to college as well, I guess it made sense. I spent the entire spring readying the home to market. With three active kids it took some major editing and a major cleanout of the basement and garage. Dylan had left an entire attic in the garage full of totally useless items. We had been in this home for twelve years, our longest stay anywhere, and had managed to accumulate stuff. When all was readied and repairs were made, I looked about and was quite happy with the results. Damn, it was clean and organized and we even had scented candles burning. Dana asked me at the time, "Why can't we always live like this?" Good question! I wondered at the time if my kids felt they were living in chaos.

With the house ready to market we took off to visit my dad and his wife in North Carolina. I didn't want to be home with all the kids when people came through to view the house. It's unnerving to hear people criticize what you think is your good taste. I optimistically planned to give it a week. Lucky us, we did find a buyer in a week and were scheduled to move at the end of the school year. After a lot of searching, I found another house and invited the kids to come and see it. At first look, they seemed a little skeptical. The house did need work, especially the ancient kitchen. As with many families, for us that was the integral part of our home, where all the action took place. There was no place for action in this tiny kitchen. I promised them I had great plans to improve it and explained what I wanted to do, bumping out walls and adding on. I also wanted to add a pool. Even though they were getting older, I was always a fan of them staying around the house with their friends rather than hanging out in other places.

The most appealing part of the home to me was the fact that it had four bedrooms; one for me, one for each of the girls when they were home, and even better, the fourth was located on the opposite side of the house from mine, over the garage. This bedroom had access through the kitchen with its own staircase. This was to be Dana's "suite" with its own bath. The best part, I thought, was that he could have total privacy, and I wouldn't have to hear all his comings and goings. In hindsight this was not the most brilliant decision on my part, but then everything was normal in my world. So I moved ahead with the offer and we got the property.

It was fun to plan with the kids the changes we were going to make to our new home. As my brothers were contractors, it wasn't long before the work was underway. The pool eventually got built. The first pool contractor turned out be somewhat of a liar, as well as totally inept at his profession. After seven long months when the job was still incomplete and the retaining walls that he had built were deemed improperly constructed, I sent him packing. He was a very large man. I grew anxious he might return, angry, so I phoned my now very good friends, the town police, for a stakeout on my home. Fortunately, he never returned. I would not be giving him referrals.

CHAPTER 9

THE HIGH SCHOOL YEARS

SHANNA WAS ABOUT to head to college and Julina was to return to her college in the fall, as well. For the first time, it would be just Dana and me in the house. Because of the renovations underway, we made our meals for the first month in a makeshift "kitchen" in the basement. It was kind of like camping out, but we thought it was funny. The house was pretty much intact other than the kitchen and family room, so life could go on somewhat normally. Because I had chosen a home close to the high school, I envisioned us having a quick breakfast and him then taking the path across the field to school. I hadn't considered the fact that many days he would be hauling his fifty-pound hockey bag with him, so making him walk was an unrealistic option. I became his driver.

In high school, as in middle school, Dana stayed organized for the most part. He continued to get good grades despite his ADHD. I attributed this to a combination of setting a structure and his participation in organized sports. By that time he was playing soccer and hockey, as well as lacrosse. He had to manage his school schedule and assignments around his sports. If he didn't finish them, there would be no sports. Sports also helped him mature as, once he had started playing ice hockey as a goalie, he had blossomed. Not being the tallest or the largest no longer mattered. His quickness and agility helped him excel and suddenly he had many good friends as teammates.

Dana's proficiency at golf was also amazing, enabling him to make the varsity golf team his freshman year in high school. Prior to this, in middle school, I would often drop him off at the local municipal golf course so he could practice. He would log in several rounds during the hours that I was off showing homes to prospective buyers. The starter, Bo, loved him and would let him make lap after lap around the course. This was the next-best alternative as we could not afford to join a country club. Dana also made his first hole-in-one there at the age of twelve. By the time he was in high school, his short game was second to none on the team.

As Dana's golf game progressed and he was now on the varsity team, he was constantly in need of rides. The municipal course was only a par-three, so this meant driving forty minutes each way, twice a day, to a county course in Scotch Plains. During the spring months, I found myself suddenly having to find an additional two and a half hours in the afternoons to juggle this driving with my work schedule. I didn't give it a lot of thought, knowing that the more Dana was involved with sports, the less likely he would be to get himself into any sort of trouble. As a typical parent I worried that my son would somehow find too much time on his hands, become bored, or fall in with the "wrong crowd." Golf is a sport that teaches values, honesty, and integrity, so I was thrilled he had taken to it and had such a passion for it. I was determined he have every opportunity to improve his skills. During his high school summers, he caddied at nearby Baltusrol Golf Club, which allowed him to have the occasional practice rounds on a course where Jack Nicklaus had won the U.S. Open. Hauling bags around the course all summer enhanced his physical fitness. He ate plenty but never gained a pound. The game was helping him grow up in so many ways.

Oddly enough, the more Dana had on his plate during high school, the better he did. He was on two ice hockey teams and had to be up most mornings by 5 or 6 a.m. to practice before school, so homework had to be done right after school. Again, he managed this well with structure. I won't say everything was perfect, far from it. Remembering things in the morning was the biggest challenge. Out the door in a hurry every day, he was bound to forget something. I can't even count the number of times I drove over to the high school with his lunch, a book, a hockey stick, or something else. I probably told myself at the time that it was my fault for not reminding him. When kids mess up, mothers try to make things right. I would continue to do so.

I looked forward to Dana's games and it thrilled and terrified me to watch him play goalie. Shanna, also a proficient ice hockey goalie, attended the games with me to cheer on her brother. I distinctly remember one game we watched where the other team intentionally tried to take him out. They successfully took him down and, as he lay unmoving on the ice, I became somewhat hysterical. I personally wanted to take out the parent whose son had done this. The other team was cheering enthusiastically as I sat there in fear for what that attack had done to Dana. Fortunately, after a bit, he recovered enough to return to the goal. We watched as his buddies took personal revenge on the one responsible for daring to harm one of their own. That's what teammates do.

Ice hockey became a way of life. It consumed every day in some fashion and every weekend. I can truthfully say that it was probably the most rewarding and memorable time of Dana's school years. Yes, he attended the junior and senior proms and had many dates. He was handsome, popular, and well liked. But the bonding between himself and his teammates was extraordinary. To this day, despite the many difficulties, some of these boys—now men—are the ones who have stuck by him as friends.

During his senior year, the team was doing exceptionally well. They had a huge game scheduled against Brick, a school in south

Jersey. The anticipation of this game was nearly consuming the boys. I hosted a team dinner the night before for all the players and coaches, serving up lasagna, salad, and crusty bread. They all sat around my family room discussing the upcoming game while they dug into their food. Even though the other team was favored, the coaches that evening were inspirational in their words and reminded them of the USA-Soviet story. Both high school coaches, Coach Nixon and Coach Simmons, were awesome in their efforts to rile the team members up and give them confidence. When asked upon his retirement in August of 2019 to single out his top two or three moments in his three decades of coaching hockey with 350 wins, Coach Nixon told a local newspaper: "The choice is an easy one, Miracle at Mennen in 2000—we beat Brick in the state semifinals, 3-2. They hadn't lost to a public school in five years. It was a huge, huge upset. It's considered one of the biggest upsets in state tournament history."

The longtime Star-Ledger sportswriter Paul Bruno also recalled that game during his interview with Nixon, twenty years after the event.

"Brick, winner of each of the last four public school state titles at the time, was the heavy favorite to skate away with its fifth state championship, but Matt Tsiang put Summit on the board first and Jeff Garibaldi scored twice in the second period—both off assists from David Haire—to extend the lead to three as Summit, then No. 11 in the Star Ledger Top 20, stunned No. 3 Brick 3-2 before an estimated 1,000 people in attendance on March 11, 2000, at Mennen Arena in Morris Township. Brad Sorrentino and Bobby Acropolis scored to cut the lead to one, but goal tender Dana Henderson stood tall with thirty-two saves to preserve what continues to be one of the biggest upsets in state history." He went on to note how the coaches fired up the boys with team printouts of the 1980 story of the US knocking off the Russians. He called Dana's play "phenomenal."

When I first read those words, written in the sports column after the game, what stood out to me was, "He stood tall." My little boy had grown up. And yes, he was phenomenal. He was no longer the little towhead that children didn't want to play with. I congratulated myself on having supported and encouraged him in his sports endeavors. By this time I had been divorced for seven years and was raising my children singlehandedly. My efforts were being rewarded with their many successes. During that time I did have a "significant other" who was supportive of me in everything I did and went with me to Dana's many games to cheer him on. He did not pretend to assume any sort of fatherly role and he never moved in with us.

During Dana's high school years there was little contact between Dana and his father. Dylan had returned from Brazil and was then living in Florida. He had married a Brazilian woman who apparently was hoping to get a US visa, because shortly after the nuptials she took off, never to return. As a result, there was never a "stepmother" for Dana to adjust to. The one time in Dana's high school career, other than his graduation, that Dylan visited his son was for the game slated after the "Miracle at Mennen" game. Yep, it even had that impact. Dylan came from Florida to watch Dana tend goal in the 1990 state championship game. Unfortunately for him and for all of us, there was to be no victory there, as Bayonne took the title. He had missed his son's moment in the sun.

With his senior year drawing to an end, Dana had decisions to make. He had applied to several colleges and finally decided to accept at Union College in Schenectady, New York. He was going to be attending with one of his long-term friends from high school and a hockey teammate. It sounded like a good plan. It wasn't too far away, and he would be able to come home for visits or I could make the trip up to visit him. His field of study was pretty much undetermined, but he thought he might pursue a business degree. Having seen both of his sisters enjoy successes in the business world, he considered this to be a viable choice.

As I was all too aware that soon I would be an "empty nester," I had decided to take all my kids (and a friend of each) on my company awards trip that spring. I was fortunate enough to have earned the trip every year since I had joined that real estate company. Dana, Julina, and Shanna had all accompanied me in 1992 on our trip to Puerto Rico when they were quite a bit younger. But this trip was to be special, as they were now older and could, with their friends, enjoy all that Bermuda had to offer. I felt that it would most likely be a long time before we could do anything like that again as a family.

The company was helping with the airfare for three, but the rest of the expense was up to me. When the kids packed, I advised them they better include some snacks. They were under no circumstances to hit the "mini bars" in the room because the charges were exorbitant. The older ones, deciding that snacks meant beer, amply filled their golf bags with six packs. I even took snacks of my own for them and left them on the tee boxes as they trailed behind my foursome. The trip was a huge success. We all had a fabulous time swimming, snorkeling, sailing, and golfing. That was the first trip we had all taken together since my divorce and it was special. Life was good. I could do this.

The day after we returned from our trip, I was scheduled to help prepare for an end-of- year graduation event for Dana's class at a local restaurant. It was the Tuesday after Memorial Day weekend, and I had just dropped Dana at school. On my way to the restaurant I received a page from my older daughter Julina. Both she and Shanna were working at the same financial company in Jersey City, where they worked in different capacities on separate floors. I immediately returned Julina's call, knowing that it must be important for her to call from the office.

"Mom," Julina answered when I called, "it's Shanna. She's had some sort of seizure."

"Seizure? What are you talking about? What happened? Is she OK?" I asked all in one breath.

"I'm not sure. I don't know," Julina cried into the phone. "They've just called the ambulance."

"Find out where they are taking her," I yelled, grabbing my keys and jacket. I went into mother motion. That's when one of your kids needs you desperately and you have to get to them as quickly as possible, and no one is to get in your way. After a few moments, Julina came back to the phone.

"Mom, the nearest hospital is right here in Jersey City. I'm told that's where they will take her. I'm going back to Shanna and stay with her."

"I'm on my way. I'll meet you at the hospital."

I was out the door in a flash and jumped into my car with my heart racing. I couldn't imagine how or why this had happened. Had I missed something? Shanna had never had anything like this happen in her life. She was twenty-two years old and had never exhibited any type of symptoms that would explain this. We had just spent a week in Bermuda and everything seemed normal. My head was reeling as I sped to Jersey City. Normally it takes over forty minutes to get there from Berkeley Heights. I made it in just over twenty. I beat the ambulance to the hospital.

I was told that no cause had been determined for her seizure. They had gotten her under control and she was then lying somewhat comfortably, and being asked several questions to determine her lucidity. As I looked around, I was less than impressed. There were wires running everywhere on the floor, and staff members seemed few and far between. She was in and out of consciousness. After a few hours, some other nurse came in to assess her. She told me that Shanna was fine and I should have her get dressed and take her home. I looked at her skeptically and asked if she was sure she was OK. The nurse assured me she was. Julina was still there with me and so together we started helping Shanna get dressed. I could tell something was off as we went about this. A moment later, Shanna suddenly started to spasm. She went into another seizure as I was holding her. I screamed for the nurse, doctor, or anyone to come and help. This momma bear was really angry at this point.

Once they had gotten her resettled, I decided to take matters into my own hands. I made some phone calls. The first was to a good friend who was a hockey parent and also a doctor. I explained the situation and where we were.

"Get her out of there," he told me.

That's what I was going to do. It was another two hours before I could make the doctor understand that I wanted my daughter released and sent by ambulance to our own nearby Overlook Hospital in Summit. Mission accomplished, we finally got her settled in there by 8 p.m. I missed Dana's sports awards dinner, the one I had been setting up for. I didn't miss many of his events, but sometimes moms have to make a choice. Shanna was released the following day. She was going to be fine and was prescribed medication to avoid subsequent seizures. This was another thing I was going to have to worry about for the rest of my life. That's what moms do.

Three weeks later, Dana's senior year came to an end. As my pool had finally been completed that spring, we decided to throw a graduation party at our house for him and all of his friends. The graduates had been accepted at a myriad of colleges and universities around the country. I wanted them to all be proud of that, so I asked each one to bring a flag or pennant from the school they would be attending. They obliged and it was so terrific to see all the pennants flying from the fence around the pool. It was a special day and one that will always remain in my heart as a reminder that once, all was good. On that day, Dana received a gift from one of his friends. It was a picture of him and his five best buddies dressed in their winter snow garb with a plaque that read, *Six Of a Kind*. It included a poem written by his friend Tim Martin.

The six boys are dressed similar
Jazzy Jackets and tailored pants
Gigantic smiles reveal their joy
As they walk linked like a chain
Not a chain that constrains
But, one which each piece is essential
The boys are parts of a puzzle
Each varied personality fitting just right

As they near their destination
Younger years flash back in their heads
College, just around the corner
New friends and unfamiliar places
Precious accomplishments and daring adventures
Their futures bright as the morning sunlight
That leaks through shades

Days of rumbling down the halls
Like a herd of cattle are diminishing
So are days of running up the sideline
After a game winning goal
Soon the chain will be broken
They will soon be on different paths

Although their lives' routes will
Depart at many different exits
For now the future can wait
'Cause the present is perfect
Six young men continue to walk together
Solid as a chain

There was so much happiness on that day and so much life to look forward to. The potential seemed limitless. Years later, having suffered through so many sorrowful experiences with Dana, that poem would serve as a painful reminder that somehow, someway, it all went so very, very wrong.

Graduation followed that Monday. Dylan did make it up for his son's high school graduation, as did Dana's grandparents. Dylan drove up in his camper, which he parked in my front yard. After I explained that he couldn't leave it there, per town rules, he eventually found another spot to hang out. It wasn't a good way to start the weekend. We were barely speaking, and he had had little to no contact with Dana or with me for months.

After the graduation ceremony, the entire family went back to my house for dinner. The conversation that evening was largely focused on what lay in store next for Dana. There was also a lot of discussion about the book John, Dana's granddad, was writing. It was called *God. com—A Deity for the New Millenium*. He had a captive audience, with all family members including my daughters in attendance. The book, we were told, was to stress the faulty logic and the harm of religions. It was about the dangers of religion and the strife it causes, based upon illogical and unproven beliefs. Given that all my children had an esteemed reverence of their granddad, they listened attentively.

I remained mostly silent. I had been raised Presbyterian and had tried my utmost to raise my children in the church. Dylan, an agnostic himself, had not participated in any of this, including being absent at Dana's baptism when he was just a baby in Brazil. The one-time Dylan did come to the church with us, Dana had been five years old and playing the role of a shepherd in the Christmas pageant. He attended Sunday school, and so had the girls, but it's hard to foster a continued belief in religion when one parent isn't on board. The kids occasionally accompanied me to church but lacked the enthusiasm for organized religion. They had been spending a lot of time with their granddad and his beliefs were clearly overriding mine. I had hoped this would change by the time they reached adulthood.

As I sat there, I felt guilt about this, too. Perhaps, I thought, I should have done more to encourage what I considered to be Christian beliefs. Maybe I didn't go to church enough. It was often difficult, as many Sunday mornings I had clients. Okay, that was no excuse. Sometimes life got in the way also, games, practices etc. At any rate, I realized that evening that I had pretty much lost the "religion battle." It seemed my role as parent was slowly being diminished. My kids were growing up. Clearly there were many influences, which I could not control, that would and could now impact their lives. I only hoped that Dana was ready to face whatever it was life would throw at him. I didn't know then how many times I would implore God to please give me the strength to get me through the challenges that were to lie ahead for both of us.

CHAPTER 10

WHERE IT BEGAN

OF COURSE, I was emotional. I was dropping off my "baby" at college, the last one to leave the nest. We had spent the entire previous month buying everything he could possibly need for his new college room. We had purchased linens, clothes, a computer, and every essential imaginable. After loading everything into my car, we made the drive up to his campus on a beautiful fall day with perfect blue skies and a refreshingly cool temperature. Dana was excited to get his room set up, but before we could drag all his stuff up to his room, there was registration. The school had arranged for the incoming freshman class to experience a weekend retreat before the beginning of the fall semester. The table for registration for this event was manned by three enthusiastic sophomore girls. It was their job to make sure all the new students were greeted and welcomed to their new environs.

We made our way over to the table through a throng of students. When Dana approached, he gave them his name and one of the girls told him he would be in the same cabin as Sarah, Emily, and Stephanie.

I looked at my son and then told the girl, with a laugh, "Well, I guess he's going to have a good time."

Dana was embarrassed. They had put him in a girls' cabin mistaking his name for a girl's. They finally got it sorted out and I told him that lots of kids were arriving that day. Guess whose name they were sure to remember? After that, everything went smoothly. We set up the basics in his room with him announcing he would do the rest when I left.

On the drive home I remember feeling sad as all parents must. I also remember thinking that this was a good thing for both him and me. He was now to be independent and make his own choices. Surely he could manage this. I had already successfully launched two children, both who were already working in the business world. They had managed their college years very well and nothing bizarre had taken place. Well, that's not exactly true if you count the time Shanna's dorm room burned and then a dumpster was dropped on her car. But we had gotten through it. Dana was with friends, would make more, and would come out a better person for the experience and knowledge he would gain. That is what I thought at the time.

In reflection, I realize that up until this point in his life I was always around him and pretty much always knew what was going on. Once I left him at college, that all changed. I could only conjecture about much of what took place during those next few years.

Dana's grades were pretty good during his freshman year. He was not playing hockey in college as his was a D-1 school. He explained to me that only the really, really good kids got to play, mostly the Canadians. I suggested that he participate in club hockey instead, and he did for a short bit. He was keen on joining a fraternity and at the end of freshman year pledged. I was worried about the potential hazing hazards every parent hears about and warned him to be careful. As it turns out, that was not what I should have been concerned about.

Dana phoned me one evening in the middle of his sophomore year. He talked about how his classes were going and about the various social functions he was setting up for his fraternity. He was the social chairman and responsible for the organization of their parties and such. He then was also playing on the ice hockey team, though not in their D-1 division. This put me at ease because in the past both the exercise and the need to maintain a schedule had helped him remain focused on his schoolwork. In addition, he was now acting as a tour guide for the Gatekeeper Honorary Society. It was his job to meet with potential new students and their parents and give them a tour of the campus.

Having filled me in on his weekly routine and commitments, he then changed the subject. He told me he had sought out a psychiatrist to talk to as he was having some difficulties with staying on focus with some of his classes. My first reaction was, *OK, that seems like a mature decision.* He's not a kid anymore and he has to be responsible for his own actions. Then he told me that the doctor, I'll call him "Dr. K," had prescribed the drug Adderall for him to take to improve his concentration.

This was the beginning of the craze when this "study drug" was prescribed by well-meaning psychiatrists. Not realizing the potential frightening addiction pattern which this drug could cause, I assumed that under the guidance of a physician, this decision was mostly likely one that would actually help Dana to successfully complete his courses. This drug was not introduced and approved by the FDA until 1996. I was not familiar with it. It wasn't until 2006 that a study was done and published in Pharmacotherapy. This journal is not typically read by the public but by the physicians themselves. They at that point recognized the prevalence and abuse of the drug on college campuses. When I researched the drug initially I did not find anything alarming. It was too soon. Today if you Google the word, you will immediately be directed to links with titles like "A warning to those who use Adderall and the like. Don't be like me," and "Adderall Horror Stories," and "The 10 stages of Adderall." I could go on and on. None of this was available then. Unfortunately, Dana has now become one of those stories.

Adderall is an amphetamine. Taken initially, the drug can help improve focus. For that reason college students, I understand, refer to it as their "study buddy." It is a legal stimulant and students use it to amp up their academic performance. It is commonly given to students with ADHD, a disorder that affects a person's ability to focus, concentrate, and be still in their own body. The condition makes it difficult to pay attention for extended periods of time. When you have this disorder, functioning mentally can feel like an impossible task. This drug is a central nervous system stimulant and increases the production of dopamine and norepinephrine in the brain. As neuroscientist Ryan Davison explains it in a video produced by the American Chemical Society: "People with ADHD tend to have lower levels of dopamine, a key chemical in the brain's reward center. This lack of dopamine means people with ADHD are constantly seeking stimulation. Amphetamines stimulate the release of dopamine and other neurotransmitters in the brain so those minor distractions don't cause you to lose focus."

While initially it may have improved Dana's performance and focus, he—like so many other students—found that the more he took, the more he craved. Whether or not he was warned this drug could be extremely addictive, I do not know. I suspect not. I conjecture that he was told a lower dose was better and it could be adjusted if necessary. Like any other drug, the body develops a tolerance. The doctor can only go by what the patient explains as symptoms and anxieties, and act accordingly. I'm sure his dosage was amped up some, as Dana probably found the dosage he was taking suddenly didn't seem to be living up to his expectations. If the dosage wasn't amped up by the prescribing doctor, of course it could be increased by the patient himself by taking more. Dana most likely told himself, "It's a legal prescription drug, right? And it's safe. It was prescribed by a doctor." I don't think in the beginning he thought he was participating in prescription drug misuse or abuse. I do understand now that he was probably enjoying the drug at that point and felt like he was soaking up information like a sponge when in class. Initially I'm sure he felt it helped tremendously.

However the scenario played out, the dosage was amped up, probably little by little and then by a lot. I did not see what was taking place. My visits with him were limited to the few times I went up to visit him for a football game weekend or his trips home. I did not detect anything amiss. When I did ask him how the drug was working, he assured me it was fine and helping him. Maybe in the beginning it was. But I was not with him daily so did not pick up on the first signs of behavioral changes. I am guessing that his friends could see what was happening and most likely had some talks with him. If so, it did not change anything. By the middle of his sophomore year the grades began to slip, but not drastically so.

Not realizing anything was wrong, I encouraged him when he suggested doing a junior year abroad as so many of his friends were planning. I learned that 60 percent of the junior class would spend some time doing an overseas program. Having traveled extensively, I felt that it would enhance his level of education to learn of a world that wasn't confined to the walls of a college campus. He mentioned Amsterdam. To this suggestion I said no. Having heard of the prevalence and availability of drugs to the general population there I suggested this was not a good choice. I had no idea at the time that he was already most likely addicted to his prescribed drug.

It was during one evening at my house that we discussed possibilities for the junior year abroad program. It was Christmastime and I was hosting a get together for my family and a lot of their friends. My kitchen was always the favorite gathering spot for all of them when they came home at Christmas. This particular evening, my daughters were there with their boyfriends. They both expressed their ideas regarding the program, much the same as mine. Everyone was drinking, including Dana. They were all of age, no problem. Having decided amongst ourselves that Budapest was a better option for his abroad study program, the conversation moved on.

Julina then announced she had hired a private investigator to try and track down her illegitimate brother or sister. This came out of nowhere. Years earlier I had told them the story of the indiscretion. She had never mentioned it to me again, so I did not know this apparently had weighed on her mind. She told us the investigator had had no luck. He didn't have enough information to go on. Dana was present at the time but wasn't paying attention as he was busy talking with his friends. I was to find out years later that he didn't remember a word of this conversation. Unfortunately, when he did find out he already had plenty of other issues to deal with.

The end of the school year arrived and Dana was busy making the arrangements for his junior year. He had applied to renew his passport and sent in all of the documents. He returned home for the summer and was successful in obtaining an internship at a large corporation, thanks to the help of one of my clients. Dana wanted to pick up some money for the ensuing year abroad. That summer it seemed like he was making progress towards responsibilities. He had a good job which he made it to on time and had money in his pocket.

The plans were all finalized for his semester abroad when he returned to school in mid-August. My friend Joe and I had decided to take a trip that month north to Maine and then onto Vermont. Right before leaving, I received a frantic phone call from Dana telling me that he still didn't have his renewed passport. Had it arrived at the house? He assured me that he had indeed sent in the documents. Knowing he was to leave within the week, I tried to figure out what to do. I called a friend in the government and asked for some help. The passport arrived, and then we had to drive it to his school in New York to ensure all the documentation was in place before he left. Of course, it was some 200 miles out of our way, but that's what moms do. It wasn't the first time, nor would it be the last, that I was running like a crazy person to make sure he got where he was going. When we arrived back home, I went up to his room and found it a chaotic mess. Thrown in a corner was a pile of unopened mail and debris. If a passport was there it wasn't likely to be found. I attributed it to his ADHD, like I had so many times before. I should have realized that this was atypical behavior for someone about to embark on a junior year abroad program.

Dana and his friend left together for JFK airport. His friend's dad drove them, so I said my goodbyes in my driveway and wished him good luck. I was assuming and hoping that the term abroad would bring nothing but good experiences for him and was delighted that he could have this opportunity. He promised to send me emails and let me know everything that was going on.

Dana was true to his word. He was great about keeping in touch, although his initial emails consisted of asking me to activate his phone card, send chargers, batteries, adaptors, and the like. For some reason, I kept all of his emails when they arrived and printed them out, thinking one day he would enjoy reading all about the places he visited and the memories he was creating. As I reread them today, I find I'm looking between the lines to see what else was going on besides his visiting eastern European capitals, classes with former CEOs from East Germany before the collapse, and trips to castles on the Rhine. In an October letter after a lengthy description about his trip to Prague, he finally answered my question about how he was feeling. I continued to be concerned about the drug Dr. K had prescribed to him.

He wrote, "Oh yeah, you asked about how I was feeling and I assume you are talking about the medicine. Dr. K was right, and it does take a few weeks before you start noticing any effects but it has definitely started working I feel like. I have been much less stressed out and considering I'm in East Germany in the ugliest most Communist looking campus I have ever seen (also the 1st) I think I have been a little more upbeat. But who knows really?"

So, it seemed that his doctor had increased the dosage of Dana's medication shortly before his departure, or maybe Dana had done so himself. I subsequently found out he had prescribed an antidepressant, as well. Regardless, there was no one to monitor his behavior, which clearly could change as a result of these prescriptions.

The emails kept coming and he kept the whole family up to date by his articulate descriptions of the cities he was experiencing. By the end of September his group had spent time in Chemnitz, Romania, the Czech Republic, East Germany, West Germany, and Vienna. I was thrilled he was recording his experiences by sending us lengthy emails every week. He spent what must have been hours composing stories about the places they went and the people they met and included detailed descriptions about palaces and castles he visited. I hoped he was being as attentive to his classes as he was in recording his travels.

As I shared his lengthy stories with the family, we decided he seemed happy and was thoroughly enjoying his experiences. Knowing that, Joe and I decided to take a trip to St John's. I needed some time off, as I had been working like a maniac. College did not come cheap. Joe had moved in with me by then. Since all my children were "launched," we felt it was time to have a life of our own. We spent an enjoyable week in the tropics and returned home rejuvenated.

My relaxation period came to abrupt end. On the drive home from the airport, we were recalling funny stories about our trip when my cell phone rang. It was my Dad's wife Jean saying that my Dad had just had a stroke. This shocked me as he was in perfect health, golfing and sailing six times a week. As soon I got in the door I raced to my computer and booked a flight down to North Carolina for the following morning.

When I arrived at the hospital I could tell he was not in good shape. He could not walk, stand, or talk. I felt totally helpless. There was nothing I could do for him. Jean, who really didn't want me to make the trip down, told me she could handle the situation and I could return home so, after a few days, I did. Thankfully, while I was there he did regain his speech. He never could walk properly again, though, and was never to play golf or sail again. While I had my concerns about Dana and this drug he had been prescribed, I decided that was not the time to burden Dad with this information. I kept it to myself.

I returned home from North Carolina and received another email from Dana on October 22. He expressed his concern about "Pops" and wanted me to be optimistic. I read over this briefly, having a lot on my mind. His email continued on to say that "with all the traveling and packing and unpacking and going from hotel to university to hotel to hotel, I managed to leave one of my medicine bottles in the hotel in Vienna. I had most of my medication in one bottle and this is the last thing I wanted to happen. I have tried so hard not to be the stupid forgetful kid that I always am and once again messed up. I know that the stuff is expensive and am quite honestly ashamed of myself for having to go through this. The antidepressant medicine (Lexapro) came in a few smaller bottles and so not all is gone. I actually have a full bottle of it and haven't checked but I think I have enough for the remainder of the trip. The ADD medicine (the Adderall) however is pretty much all gone. As you know the prescription has to be made out by Dr. K and I was hoping you could call him and explain the situation. I know this sounds trite, but I promise I am trying to learn from these stupid mistakes and I will make sure this never happens again. I know the worst part is that the medicine isn't cheap and it's completely unfair to you to have this sort of thing happen. The fact is though, this is day fifty-two of one hundred and there is still a ton of time and work left to be done here and I really need to have this refilled. I know that I have been completely tapping your resources and I promise I'm going to do my best to make this up to you."

He also went on to say he was sending a letter to me, which I received later. In the letter he thanked me for "being such a great mother and for putting up with all my chaos with such a calm." He went on to say, "I know I am not good at showing my appreciation, but I want you to know how grateful I am to have you as my mom. It amazes me seeing how busy you are and how much you have on your plate, and how you go about every day with such ease and calm."

When I read these words I was touched, as any mother would be. I was also very forgiving–most likely too forgiving. No matter what Dana did, he always had a way of letting me know how sorry he was and how much he loved me. And while I knew he did, he also manipulated me so very well.

When I received the email, I called the doctor to refill his prescription. You see, I believed what he had written me. Perhaps it was true. Perhaps he did lose the medicine. Years later, I came to believe he had again amped up his dosage himself while abroad to cope with all the travel, classes, and papers that were due. Maybe if I had not just returned from visiting my ailing father I might have had a clearer mind. When I realized years later that I had saved all of his emails from that time, I reread them and the light dawned that this was most likely one of the most blatant warnings I had received.

It wasn't three days later that I received another email. This time he informed me that he had been at a club the evening before and his jacket was stolen—with his wallet in it. He was informing me that he had in it the credit card I had given him "for emergency purposes." He wanted me to cancel it immediately. He did still have his debit card and his driver's license. He wasn't asking for money, just to cancel the card. He went on to implore me to not tell his friend's parents, who also lived in town and whom Dana was traveling with. I wondered at the time why not, but then Dana went on to explain that "he didn't want his friend to know as the two of them were not getting along so well." I thought that was strange at the time. Later I realized that his friend most likely knew exactly what Dana was getting into and did not approve or endorse it.

Two days later I received a call from the credit card company. I explained I had given it to my son for emergency purposes only, and he told me it had been stolen. They then informed me there was a large charge on it which definitely could not be defined as "emergency purposes." The card evidently had not been stolen. The charge was not one of Dana's finest decisions. I was shocked to find out that it was for costs at a strip club. What right minded son puts a charge for a strip club on his mother's credit card? I assumed he had been drinking and didn't realize what he was doing. I suppose I chalked it up to "boys will be boys," but was unnerved by how thoughtless and stupid his act was. It was so uncharacteristic of the son I knew that I should have been more attuned. I still don't know if his jacket was actually stolen, and I don't care. It has now become clear that the decisions he was making abroad were not all good ones.

It was shortly after this incident, at the beginning of November, when Julina and I decided to take a quick trip to Budapest over the Thanksgiving weekend to visit Dana. We knew he was missing the family a lot. This was the first time he had been away from home for any extended period of time, away from family. I don't remember at the time thinking I had to "check up" on him. I was curious to see where he was studying and had never been to Budapest. He was excited we were coming. We flew over and spent just three nights there. We took him and his friends out to dinner, walked over the Chain Bridge at night, toured the city, and had a great time. He seemed happy and healthy, though a bit on the thin side. When I mentioned this to him he assured me it was all the traveling around and studying for his classes that had worn him down a bit. I asked him about his most recent exam. Two weeks before he had written me that at 1:15 a.m. he was starting to study for it. The exam was to be at 9 a.m.

"No worries though, it's going to be cake," he had assured me.

I wasn't so sure. He had failed his econ exam the week before. Dana told me that he had spoken to his professor about it and explained it off as being worried about his grandfather and how it had really gotten to him. The professor empathized, changed the weight of the exam, and allowed Dana to do a paper to compensate. I thought that was rather compassionate. I then reminded him the end of the term was approaching and he couldn't let his grades slide. He told me "things aren't looking too bad." I left him in Budapest not realizing all was not right. He was to arrive home in about three weeks.

Dana was flying into LaGuardia Airport in New York. This airport has been under construction for approximately twenty-five years and still hasn't improved. It's a nightmare to get around and there's nowhere to park. It is not a fun place to go. As much as I was looking forward to seeing him, I was not relishing the thought of dealing with the congested traffic and incessant horn blowing. I drove around the arrivals area a few times waiting for him to come out. When I finally saw him, I was taken aback. I could tell something was wrong. He more or less staggered toward the car and got in, clutching his stomach and saying he didn't feel well. He was shaking. He then told me had gotten confused coming out and almost was run over by a truck. When I noticed he only had one duffel bag with him, I surmised we had a problem. He confessed he had left one bag inside by mistake and was trying to go back and get it but they wouldn't let him reenter. Unsure about what to do next, I suggested I park the car and we go together to try and locate it, but Dana insisted we needed to leave and go home. He looked haggard and tired, so I decided to make for home and follow up with the bag later. He then informed me that all his money was in his other bag. Great! I knew there was no way he would ever see that again. When I asked him about his stomach, he told me it was probably something he ate on the plane.

Dana went directly to bed when we arrived home. I made some calls and did manage to locate his other duffel bag. I asked the baggage claim people to please send it to Newark, where I would pick it up the next day. Shanna said I shouldn't, that Dana should drive in and get it himself. But even the next day he was in no condition to drive, so of course I did. No, the money was no longer in his bag. The holiday season was not starting out well.

Now that he was home, I was curious to see if Dana would make good on his promise to help out around the house more to repay me for some of the debt he had incurred. He had promised this in one of his more recent letters. He wasn't very well that vacation, so the promise went unfulfilled. I encouraged him to just rest and try and get healthy for the next semester. He eventually improved by the end of the holidays and returned after the first of the year to his school to resume his studies. Once again, I was forced to monitor him from afar.

That spring of Dana's junior year, Joe and I drove up to pay him a visit. The conversation mostly centered on how his fraternity had lost their house and now it was being trashed. He was going to have to find another place to live his senior year. We all set out to play golf somewhere that Saturday, but Dana got completely lost on our way there. I thought this was strange because I knew he had been there before. After turning around at least three times, we finally found the course. I guess I thought his meds weren't working that day. The underlying problem was that every time he got confused or forgetful, I contributed it to his ADHD. He made it through the rest of the school year but his final grades were mediocre.

When Dana returned home for the summer, he decided to go back to Baltusrol Golf Club to caddy. He said he could make more money doing that than anything else. Unfortunately, he didn't get called upon often enough to make it worthwhile, so it probably wasn't the best choice. That summer he also was trying to qualify for a golf state standing by playing in different tournaments. On one such occasion, after a two-hour drive to find the course, he arrived home early totally distraught. He had gotten lost and lost his spot in the competition. This was totally uncharacteristic of him. Golf was important. I should have detected at the time that his behavior was erratic. I suppose at the time I attributed it to just another "Dana moment." That summer there was no real structure in his schedule, which was not good. He didn't seem to be focused on much of anything. I tried to get him refocused but without a structured scheduled this was difficult. We muddled through the summer trying to create normal.

An interesting conversation took place that summer which caused me to decide that perhaps we weren't quite the "normal" family I had thought us to be early on. All my kids were home for the weekend and one Saturday evening we were all gathered on the patio having a pre-dinner cocktail. For some reason, the conversation turned to passports. The girls had for years hounded me with questions about their passports. They always wanted to know why there were so many stamps on them. My answer was always the same, "We traveled a lot." We had friends all over South America and when we traveled from South America to the US for our home leave we would make visits to Colombia, Bogota, Venezuela, Rio, or wherever our friends were currently posted. After my response they would typically look at each other and roll their eyes. It happened again.

"What?" I said. "What is your point in asking this time and again?"

"Mom? Have you even seen our passports?" they both asked.

"No, your father always kept them when we traveled. It was easier that way. Have you even seen them?"

"Yep," they both answered. And then they laughed.

"OK, what is the big deal here, girls?" Now I was beginning to feel like they were in on a secret joke. They were now treating me like I was some sort of moron.

Then Julina explained. "Remember last Christmas when we all were up in New York and Dad came to visit?" I did. I went to bed early that night, not wanting to endure a long drawn out conversation with the man.

"Yes, and?"

"Well, last year he decided that now we should all have our own passports back as we were older, so he gave them to us."

"And?" I asked.

"And we both looked at them and there are like twenty stamps there." They then pulled the passports out and handed them to me. They looked at me expectantly. I felt like I was somehow being tested.

"Are you going to pretend now, Mom, that you didn't know anything about this? All this time we have asked you about this and your answer was, 'we traveled a lot.'"

I then looked through their passports. "Oh my God," I said. "You're right. There are so many stamps here to places we never took you. I don't get it."

"Really, Mom? You still say you don't know anything about this?"

"No, I don't, girls. I don't get it."

They looked at each other in disbelief. "I really don't think she knows," Shanna said to Julina.

"Knows what?"

"Well, Mom, we didn't understand it either so we asked Dad last Christmas. That's the night you went to bed early. We confronted

Dad with these and asked him how it was that there were so many stamps. He realized that his excuses weren't going to fly with us. So he explained it."

"Explained what?"

"Well, I guess when we were living in Brazil he met a friend who worked with the consulate." That would be the aforementioned friend, Peter. "They became friends and Dad was asked if he would consider doing undercover work for the CIA. They felt he would be perfect as he spoke fluent Spanish and Portuguese and traveled extensively anyway. He told us when he traveled he would gather information about 'people of interest' he met on his flights and in his travels and report back to them. When he traveled, he took our passports as well and told the authorities he was traveling with his family. That's why there are so many stamps."

This was news to me. I was married to the man for twenty-three years and this was a secret I had not known. The indiscretion, yes. The CIA undercover work, a definite no. I had no clue about his part-time job. I was stunned.

"You didn't know, Mom?"

"No, I certainly didn't. And now I feel like a complete idiot."

"Mom, don't. We have to tell you this. When we confronted Dad about it, he actually told us you never knew but we didn't believe him. But we thought that might be true when he told us he didn't hide the money he earned, but deposited it into your joint account. He never told you about the money he said. He never lies about money."

I don't remember much what was said after that. It seemed that my life was beginning to read like a soap opera. You read stories about women who have been deceived and think, *How could she not have seen that?* I realized that woman was now me and I was reeling from the information. My first thoughts were, *What else have I missed? I guess I am not as astute in perceiving behaviors as I had thought myself to be.* At that moment I felt a bit of my self-confidence slipping away, but I was determined not to show it. Needless to say, this latest revelation did nothing to enhance my opinion of my secretive ex. I resolved that I would have to be more attentive to family matters if I were to succeed as a single mom.

The summer came to an end and to my great relief no other family secrets were unearthed and no more drama played out. It was time to get Dana back to school for his final year of college—the year that would, at its end, finally grant me some financial freedom.

September arrived and he returned to campus, where he muddled through his courses. If I had to guess, this is when he continued to amp up the dosage of his meds and started doctor-shopping in order to obtain the drugs his body craved. The effects may have been apparent to his friends at school, but not to me. Perhaps he was just really good at hiding them. But eventually the meds got the better of him. His inability to focus on important details would contribute to his failure to graduate.

Whatever was going on with him clearly caused this disappointment. I realized much later, after examining all the evidence that had been in front of me all the time, that this was most likely inevitable. Either I didn't pay enough attention, or maybe he was just that good at deceiving.

My girls had warned me several times that they thought he was on drugs. I had always responded that he was. He had ADHD, was under a doctor's care, and was taking a prescribed drug. I didn't realize it was addictive and how it was already ruining his life. Most importantly, I did not realize the extent of the problem. At the time I thought his failure to graduate was simply a matter of not having contacted the school where he took his summer course the end of his freshman year, and getting that course transferred to his school. So what did I do when he returned home that fateful spring? I continued to help him.

Dana needed a job. In my career I was most fortunate to meet many great people who would become wonderful friends. To this day I owe them a great debt and also a lot of apologies. They helped both me and Dana out so many times. This was one of those times

I called on one of these friends. He was a client I had sold a house to, and I became close friends with him and his wife. He had a very high position in a large insurance company in the city. I called him and explained that while Dana had actually earned his degree in economics, he hadn't exactly graduated with the class and didn't have a diploma to show for it. Was there any way he could help find Dana a position in his company? And he did. In fairness, Dana had obtained another job offer on his own from Cantor Fitzgerald, the company which had lost so many of its employees in the attack of September 11, three years prior. They were still hiring. He had already accepted that job but, after reconsidering, decided that this other company perhaps offered him a better opportunity. I don't think in the end it would have made a difference as to what would follow.

He was offered the position on August 16. I remember I was taking the day off to play golf with him when he received the call, and I was elated! I recall jumping up and down on the green after hugging him. After the extreme disappointment of not seeing him graduate, I began to think that maybe it would all turn out for the best after all. Diploma or not, he was fortunate to get this great offer. Later that week we went shopping together to outfit him for his new job. I was just so proud of him.

The proud momma wasn't so proud the following week. It seemed any semblance of elation I experienced was destined to be followed by bad news. He informed me that he had to pay a fee to the Municipal Court and several fees for parking tickets. What was wrong with him? He had no money coming in yet. These fell to me to pay. I also was settling his account for the apartment he had rented with his friends at school and money was still owed on that. Then I had to write a check to his Dr. K. who did not know how dramatically he had changed Dana's life. But, I was trying to be optimistic. It would work out. Once he had an income of his own, all that would change.

He started his job in September and professed to enjoy it, although he didn't seem thrilled with his immediate boss. He hung in there, though, and finally received his first paycheck. He actually gave me a check for $400 as a start to pay me back for some of the money he owed me. The check bounced. He had many friends and spent a lot of time in the city after work going out with them. Entertainment in NYC is not inexpensive, and it seemed he was spending a lot of money—more than he was making, I later found out. Knowing he was generous with his friends, I tried not to lay too much fault at his feet but rather tried to explain how he needed to start to budget his money. He promised to try.

As we settled into our fall routine, I decided that year to host Thanksgiving for the entire family. My dad was somewhat mobile and I looked forward to him and his wife joining us. I also had invited the friend who had helped Dana secure his job. As this man was German, I was a little apprehensive at the time, my Dad having served in WWII. I needn't have worried. The friend fortuitously wore a white sweater with a large American flag on it. We all observed as they became fast friends, talking for hours. About thirty of us enjoyed Thanksgiving together that year, my brothers and their wives, and all their kids as well as all of my kids. It was to be the last Thanksgiving we spent together.

The holidays came and went. Dana was living at home with me as he had no means yet to get his own place. I figured that would come with time. As I mentioned before, Joe was also living with me at the time. When he had first moved in, Dana was away at school. Now he was back at home. At first, the living situation was good, but then eventually they did get on each other's nerves. Looking back, it seemed that Dana was never particularly happy when someone else decided to take up residence in our home. At one point it got bad enough that I did ask Joe to move out. I couldn't stand the conflicts and I hated choosing sides. Now it was just the two of us again.

From January through the spring, Dana was up at the crack of dawn for the commute to NYC every day. Then he began to complain of back issues. He said that at work he had to sit for long periods in a chair, and that it was uncomfortable. He had asked if the people at work could find him a different chair, but apparently that wasn't going to happen. Then one day in April, I got a call on the house phone, which I actually answered. I didn't usually, because I used my cell phone pretty exclusively figuring anyone who called the house phone was most likely a solicitor. This time it wasn't. It was Dana's boss wanting to know where he was. I told him that, as far as I knew, Dana had gone in to work. While I was speaking with him, I walked up to Dana's room to find him in bed. I then handed the phone to him. I decided it was his problem at this point and Mom wasn't going to get involved. Dana got up and hurriedly dressed, telling me he had overslept. I don't remember that happening again, but it certainly didn't set well with his boss.

That year was very busy for me. It was 2005 and I was still working like crazy as the real estate market was then booming. In the spring I bought a condo on Hilton Head Island, South Carolina, which I thought would be a great place for us all to use when we could, and rent out when we weren't using it. I flew down there to get it ready and spent two weeks painting, buying furniture, and doing everything else it needed to make it rentable. Now that Dana had a job, I was sure that he would want to use it occasionally as well. That same year Shanna moved to her new house which I had sold her, and of course that was time consuming in a good way.

Our calendar seemed full constantly. Early in the fall, Dana's friend, the one who had been adopted in Brazil, got married and our entire family went to that affair as well. I was enjoying my kids all becoming older and getting to experience knowing them as adults. Then Shanna became engaged and we had a wedding to plan. I was delighted beyond words. It was turning out to be a very good year.

September 29 ended all of that. Dana called me from work, very upset. He had been fired. When I asked why, he said he really didn't know. Of course, he said his boss was an asshole and for some reason didn't like him. Not having any clue why this had happened, I felt surely there had been some mistake. I was wrong. He said he was catching the next train home, so I drove to the station to pick him up ready to console or ask questions. He didn't even want to talk, but came home, threw himself on the sofa, and just cried.

The next weeks were not fun. Dana was depressed, I was depressed, and I couldn't figure out a way to help him or make things better. Because that's what moms do. They try to make things better. The problem was, I didn't understand the problem so there was no way I could make it better. There was so much I didn't know then. I did know he was going to have to find some kind of work because I was not going to support him forever. After a few days of letting him get over misery, I shared this with him. I talked to my boss and he said Dana could help out at the office on weekends. That was a start. Well, that lasted about four or five weeks because Dana would take off and not come back at the time he was supposed to.

Dana sent his resume to a lot of places and had some interviews, but unfortunately had no luck until he eventually got a job waiting tables at a local restaurant. That wasn't exactly what I had in mind when I paid all those tuition bills for his very expensive college. I assumed at the time that this setback was only temporary. I knew lots of people who had been let go from their jobs but bounced back with resilience and found another. This did not happen. While Dana worked as a waiter, he continued to look for something more lucrative and related to his college degree. One afternoon he finally received his diploma in the mail from the school. It was somewhat of an anticlimactic moment when it arrived, as Dana simply put it on the shelf.

Dana continued working at the restaurant throughout the fall and then into the winter. He was not earning great deal of money. Most of his expenses at this point were being paid by me. He did have his own car which I had gotten for him at the end of high school. Rent was free as he was living with me. I was paying for his health and car insurance. What money he earned he should have been able to save. Yet he never seemed to have any. I guess I didn't really think much about it at the time. I was busy trying to plan my daughter's wedding, which was to take place the following fall.

By the spring of 2006 I could see that his attempts at finding a position were futile. I suggested that since this didn't seem to be working out, perhaps he should consider going to a golf school. He had always loved the game and with his golf proficiency maybe he could make a career of it. After weighing the options we decided that he would go to the San Diego Golf Academy in Myrtle Beach. Again, I called on another friend whom I knew had a second home in Myrtle Beach. She had a guest cottage behind her house and I asked if she would consider renting it out to Dana while he attended the school there. She agreed and so Dana now had a place to live. I paid his first semester tuition to the tune of $5,500. His intent was to take a student loan for the remainder of the program, as he didn't want me to incur any more expenses on his behalf. For so many reasons, that loan was never repaid.

CHAPTER 11

CRAZINESS

DANA HEADED OFF to Myrtle Beach in August. I bade him farewell and good luck, again. I was in the middle of gutting my bathroom, as it had suddenly sprung a leak, not surprising considering it was circa 1940. My brothers were called in to make it habitable and told to try and not break the bank in renovations as I had a lot on my plate. I was then off to my daughter's engagement party in Connecticut. From there I drove down to Hilton Head to finalize the plans for Shanna's wedding, which was to be held there in November. Since I was already south, I decided I may as well stop in Myrtle Beach to make sure Dana had settled in. He had, and he had decided he didn't like the paint in the cottage so he had taken it upon himself to repaint it. I can't say he did a great job. This wasn't to be the only time he would lose himself in paint projects. At the time I thought it was commendable to take that upon himself—yet another sign I missed.

Initially, the golf program was going well for him. He made a lot of new friends and was enjoying doing what he loved most, golf. I told him he would have to get some part-time work while down there to cover his expenses and he did. At first, he worked as a greenskeeper and had to get up early in the morning to put in his hours before

classes. That did not work out so well, so he quit. Then he decided
that he would get a job as a waiter in one of the restaurants, as he
already had experience. That seemed like a much better choice and
that position he was able to keep. The job worked out well for him,
but his choice of new friends there was questionable. What went on
in Myrtle Beach, I had no idea but could only guess. I came to believe
that all of the prominent tee shirt shops are nothing more than drug
fronts. Just saying. It was years until I found out all that did take place
in Myrtle Beach, none of it good.

One evening Dana called me saying that he had had difficulty in
getting into his house and for some reason had to get into my friend
Sandy's adjoining house to get another key. In trying to get through
the window, he had accidently broken it. I found out later it was a very
large and expensive window. Dana said he would pay for it which of
course didn't happen. My friend was pretty unhappy with the situation
and rightfully so. She decided that Dana needed to find a place to
live somewhere else. I apologized profusely. She is yet another friend
to whom I owe many thanks but, because of Dana's actions, has not
spoken to me since that event. I can't say that I blame her.

Shortly after his eviction, Dana reached out to some of his
friends and four of them decided to rent an apartment together.
He was totally pleased with his new apartment because now he had
an internet connection, which he hadn't had before, and a proper
kitchen to cook in. His former place was little more than one room
with a mattress and a desk. I drove down to Myrtle Beach to help
him get situated in his new digs. I also wanted to see the apartment
I had just helped pay for and meet his friends. In addition, I needed
to sort out with him several bills which I had just paid. They had
arrived in the mail at my house in New Jersey. Knowing he didn't
have the resources, I just paid them off. They included several from
Banana Republic, a traffic ticket, and a payment to the IRS. I knew
they would not wait. I also paid for his rent in Myrtle Beach and
his health insurance. He said he would pay me back. At the time,

I was concerned about his credit and was trying to keep it in good standing. This also would turn out to be a futile situation. I suggested that perhaps he try getting a job selling Christmas trees during the holiday season to earn some extra money. He told me they didn't have Christmas trees in Myrtle Beach. Not having lived in South Carolina yet, I believed this. What was I thinking!?

In November, Dana attended Shanna's wedding which was held on Hilton Head Island. Months of planning had gone into this family event and Dana was to be one of the groomsmen. He was thrilled to be a part of this major family gathering. My dad was able to attend with his wife, as well as Ruth and John, Dana's other grandparents. Dana's dad also attended. We went the nontraditional route with both of us walking with Shanna. Originally it was planned to have only me, but, well, he was her dad. The wedding went off without a hitch. It took place on the beach with dolphins frolicking in the waves behind us. The weather was perfect with blue skies and eighty-degree temperatures despite it being November. A cocktail party ensued to the tunes of a steel band and was followed by a sit-down dinner and dancing. Dana cheerfully interacted with everyone and seemed relaxed and positive.

At no time during that week did anyone mention noticing anything strange regarding Dana's behavior. I will say, though, that none of them had been around him for any time at all since the "pseudo-graduation." In fact, I believe that is the last time any of the family had been with Dana since then. If anyone should have picked up any strange behavior it should have been me, but I was totally focused on the wedding. I would prefer to believe that perhaps it wasn't only me he was capable of deceiving. He was really quite good at it. He returned to Myrtle Beach and to his golf program and to Lord knows what else.

I returned home to prepare for Julina's wedding, which was planned for the following year in Vermont. Again, the whole family was to be in attendance, along with many, many friends. When the wedding weekend arrived, Julina and Doug paid for Dana's plane ticket to fly up. He came with a then-girlfriend. Here's the thing.

Dana always had a girlfriend. Despite his circumstances, there was always someone with him. They didn't last.

There was a lot of chaos during that wedding weekend involving Dana. He was never where he was supposed to be. At one point during the weekend, he had taken the car that Julina's dress was in. We were all looking for him, as it was vital to locate the dress. The cell phone reception was non-existent in the mountains and keeping tabs on his location became a challenge. In spite of the chaos created by him, though, the wedding was a huge success. It also took place outdoors against the backdrop of the changing fall colors of the mountain. I now had two married, one to go. That last would be Dana. Would that ever happen? I suspected not soon because by the end of the weekend he and his girlfriend had gotten into an argument. I knew it had something to do with money. I assumed that she had lent Dana some and not been repaid. By the end of the weekend they were not speaking. That is the last I saw of her.

By 2008 he had been in the golf program for almost two years. Even though he seemed to be enjoying the program and benefiting from it, I was beginning to feel that this was not the best choice for him. He was complaining about how some of the courses were such a waste of time. I was ever hopeful that perhaps he had found his niche and could make a living in some capacity in the golf industry. This was not to be.

Early that year I received a phone call from his roommate Chase telling me Dana had gone to the hospital. Now what? I immediately called the hospital to see what was going on, and they told me he was in intensive care and something about excruciating pain. He had driven there the evening before after leaving work, and just left his car in the parking lot and gone to the ER. I finally managed to speak with him. He was rambling on about how nice one of the nurses was. She had even given him ice cream! He did not seem especially lucid, so I immediately booked a flight down. When I arrived at the hospital I went straight to his room and found a gaunt sickly person clearly in a great deal of pain. Apparently, the doctors had performed surgery on him but would not elaborate on the details, stating it was a privacy issue. Years later I would learn that my son had epididymitis, an inflammatory condition that can be acute or long term. He had had an acute attack caused by long-term use of drugs. This condition would persist for years.

After I had spent a short time with him in his hospital room, one of the nurses came in and said he needed to get up and walk around. I told her I didn't think that was such a good idea by the looks of him, but she insisted. I helped him out of bed and took his arm so we could have a walk around the corridors. Halfway down the first hallway he grasped at his stomach. I could see that he was now bleeding profusely through the bandages. Trying not to panic, I called the nurse and showed her what was happening. She reluctantly agreed he should go back to bed. As soon as I got to the room I called my father-in-law John who was an abdominal surgeon and explained what was going on. John called the hospital to check on his grandson and eventually he received better treatment. He stayed in the hospital for three days. I remained long enough to see Dana resituated in his apartment after restocking it with provisions. His roommates promised to look after him and see that he had what he needed. I would have stayed longer but they assured me they had it well under control. They did not.

Calmness in life eluded me. I learned in January, just prior to Dana's hospital incident, that my dad had cancer. He went to a facility in Philadelphia and stayed there for perhaps a week. The staff recommended that he go to an assisted living facility where he could be treated and cared for without having to depend on his wife and family. He wanted no part of that. Jean, his wife, said he would come home with her and she would care for him. Jean still had her home in New Jersey which she kept after her first husband died, so she took Dad there rather than to their home in North Carolina. Part of this decision was because two of my brothers and I lived in New Jersey at that time. As soon as Dad returned to her home from the hospital, Jean told

the family that she now had to go in for an immediate surgery. As my
brother Jim and I lived the closest, it was decided that we would rotate
in two-day shifts to care for Dad. Unfortunately, Jean had complications
and was not able to return home for weeks. In the interim my Dad
worsened, quickly. It was now up to us to figure out what to do. He
would have no part of a nursing home and we respected that. My third
and youngest brother Steve and his wife decided to have Dad come
and stay at their home. Because all my brothers were proficient with
tools, they immediately set about building a handicap ramp for the
house and revamping the downstairs so that Dad would have privacy
and the family around him. We were all totally focused on making
him comfortable.

All of this took place at the same time I had to fly to Myrtle
Beach. I should have been much more attuned to what was going on
there with Dana. Unfortunately, his hospitalization coincided with
my dealing with my Dad's terminal illness. It was not starting out to
be a very good year, and things just got worse. I went every few days
to visit my Dad, an hour and a half away. He worsened and hospice
was called in. He eventually died in April. Jean was finally able to
come home and see him just three days before he died. I felt like
an orphan. Perhaps most people do when they have lost both their
parents, regardless of their age.

Dana did come home for the funeral. I paid for a ticket for him
to fly up. I was too caught up in my grief to even remember his state
of mind at the time. He was very concerned about me, which was
not unfounded. In addition to my dad's passing, I was increasingly
concerned about the slumping real estate market. To compound
this, the bills for Dana kept coming in. First there were hospital
bills. While I had been paying for his medical insurance, not all the
charges were covered for his recent hospitalization.

In addition, Dana never seemed to have money for his rent. Here
is where the signs should have been so obvious. I had agreed to cosign
a lease with him for the apartment he was now renting in Myrtle

Beach. His credit at this stage was anything but commendatory. He had also convinced me that the car he had been driving since high school was too expensive to repair. He explained that even the seat belt didn't work which he found out would be very costly to replace. He suggested it would be better to lease a car so that the maintenance bills wouldn't continue to be a financial drain. At the time it seemed like a reasonable idea so I agreed. He sold the other car for what he could get and he, with my help, leased a car. I now was on the hook for both his rent and car. Of course, promises were made that not one payment would be late. I pressed upon him the importance of this because of my credit and I didn't want to lose my own good standing.

Several months later I received a copy of my less than commendatory credit report and sent an email to Dana saying, "I just got a copy of my credit report and the only two late payments I have had in TWENTY YEARS are for YOUR CAR and YOUR RENT. (Need I remind you that I am the cosigned on that lease?) DON'T BE LATE on any, Dana. It is imperative I keep this credit in good standing!"

I felt at the time that was ample warning. I was so wrong. I did not know this was just the beginning. I had already made his August and September rent payments. Apparently, he didn't want to tell me he was behind on the rest as well. As if that weren't enough, I had collected a myriad of bills from the postman who kept appearing at my front door and was faced with the problem of what to do with them. I knew it would be an exercise in futility forwarding them to Dana. I considered the options and decided to pay them off to try and maintain some sort of credit stability for him. My checkbook tells me I wrote checks for his expenses in the amount of $3,709 that year. Did I mention that didn't include his tuition? At the time I felt it was the right thing to do. I was optimistic that he would graduate this golf program and finally secure a job, and that he would have the financial means to repay me.

Then that same summer, his granddad John died. Dana and he had been very close. In fact, they spoke much more often than he and his father. The funeral was not to be held until November as it was to be at Arlington National Cemetery, as John was a retired Air Force colonel. He was also the "go to" for advice for all of my children. It became a family joke that whenever one of the girls would call for medical advice on an issue, his first question to them was "Are you pregnant?" He was never one to beat around the bush and he was always there for his grandkids. Dana took his death hard, as we all did. I realized that the one other person Dana could go to for help or advice besides me was now gone. To his credit, Dana made an amazing DVD for the Celebration of Life ceremony. I believe it was his therapy. The relatives were all impressed and asked for copies of it. Dana did have a lot of artistic talents when he put his mind to it. This was one of his better moments at this phase of his life.

Dana didn't finish golf school. By December he announced he wanted to come home. He said he was having misgivings about the lifestyle of the people he was with and now didn't feel he wanted to pursue a career in golf or the golf industry. He told me he was going to come home and put his resume out there again and see if he could find a job in the business world again. He felt it was a much better option. Shortly after receiving this news I received an email from my ex saying that Dana had called him and told him he was planning to quit the golf program and move back in with me. He said he had forced himself to listen and not say a lot but, in short, he said that Dana was not making much sense as far as he could make out. He expressed his concerns and said he would appreciate my thoughts and suggestions on how he might be of help. He told me also that he thought he had an idea of what might be going on. At the time I dismissed this whole email, because how on earth would he have any idea what was going on when he had not been around for years? This was one of the rare times when he and Dana had actually talked. Unfortunately, Dylan and I did not.

Dana drove home right before Christmas. I was decorating my home as I always did with lights on the bushes, swags on my fence, and candles and wreaths in the windows. I loved decorating for Christmas and was thrilled when Dana decided he wanted in on the action. He took off to the hardware store, returning with what seemed like miles of stringed lights. When I asked what he was going to do with them he told me he was going to put lights on all the branches of the trees around my house. Feeling that was rather enterprising of him, I agreed. An hour passed and he was off to the store, again. Then, while I was inside baking, I heard a clatter on the roof. Knowing it wasn't Santa, I went out to investigate. Dana was literally running around on the roof stapling lights all over it.

"Dana, what in the hell are you doing?" I yelled up at him.

"Decorating, Mom! I'm going to cover the entire roof with lights! The trees, too! It's going to look awesome!" He had gotten the idea from some show he had seen on TV. He then told me he had to go back for more lights.

I did appreciate his enthusiasm, but the bizarreness of his behavior escaped me. Our home remained a sight to behold during the Christmas season. The outlandishness of the lighting was confirmed by my friend Maggie who arrived surprisingly on time at my home with her daughter for a New Year's Eve party. She had never been good at directions and always managed to get lost when trying to find my house. When she arrived at my door she was laughing hysterically.

"Oh my God! No getting lost this time! You could see your house from the space shuttle!"

I explained how Dana had volunteered his time and efforts to decorate and this was the result. Wasn't it grand? The neighbors all commented on how festive it looked. What they said amongst themselves, I had no clue. It was two months after the holidays when he finally removed the lights. He told me he couldn't get the staples out from the roof, so he just cut all the lights strands. So much for frugality.

Having him home again with me was a challenge. I explained that he was going to have to get a job while he looked for something in the business world. I seemed to say that often to him, right? Because he already had a lot of restaurant experience, he went to work for a more upscale restaurant in town where he knew he would be able to make better money. He continued to send out his resume, and I called up all my friends to see if they could help find him a position. His sisters also were on the lookout for him, offering up suggestions. Dana was scouring the internet and did come up with a possibility of a job in Florida. It had something to do with booking tee times. I paid (of course) for him to fly down and interview, but he didn't get the job. Then finally he did get a job offer in March with a large firm in New York. The human resources people were to contact him by the end of the week. We waited. When he didn't hear from them, he called them and learned they had decided to rescind the offer. I suspect it was because of his bad credit, in spite of what I had done to try and preserve it. He was resigned to continue working as a waiter. He threw himself into his job and seemed surprisingly happy at what he was doing, even offering to make planting boxes for the restaurant in which they could grow their own herbs. This is when the building phase started.

By the end of January he complained he was not feeling well. He had been to his doctor several times, but that doctor could not find anything specifically wrong so decided to send him to a cancer specialist. He was sent for several ultrasounds at the hospital and, when I met him there later, he told me that three doctors had been there before me but they didn't have much to say. We went home to await the results of his tests. He got his results back by February 11 and was told no cancerous cells had been found. I related this good news to the family, who had all been concerned. They too wondered what was going on. After he was feeling better, he decided to go back to work.

Though his job was steady, he was not earning a great deal of money. My daughters knew by this time that I had been paying Dana's bills and expressed their concern that there was no way he was going to be able to pay me back. Shanna sent me an email suggesting that I talk to Dana about declaring bankruptcy. I told her I had already spoken to

Dana about this and had looked up the possible ramifications of that option. I explained to him that it didn't have the stigma it once did, especially considering that most of the debt was incurred by medical bills. At this point I estimated he probably owed about $20,000. Shanna encouraged me not to pay any more of his bills because it was "sucking away everything you have and it's not going to get better. It's not fair to you."

Dana did not declare bankruptcy. I was still not sure it was the best idea. I should have listened to many people at the time, but I think I was too determined to "fix things" myself. I was just too independent to heed the advice of others, and I wasn't sure that my daughters knew best. Wasn't I supposed to be the mother, the decision maker? Somehow everything had suddenly gotten out of whack.

In retrospect, I could have used a better support system at the time. I found myself sharing stories of Dana's behaviors with two of my dearest friends, both of whom worked in real estate with me. They both had older children and I felt they were qualified to offer the best advice. By this point in my life I didn't have any real contact with those Summit moms with whom I had shared many hockey games. Their sons were all off to good jobs, meaningful relationships, and some of them were even buying their own homes. I felt like Dana's life paled in comparison. I guess I just didn't want to hear their sympathy on how things weren't working out for him.

I didn't speak to my brothers much on the subject either. Steve was quite a bit younger, and Jim had no children. My older brother, who was living in Vermont, would have, in hindsight, been the person to talk to. I didn't reach out, though, because I wanted him to think his little sis had everything under control. I was the one who had managed to move her family around the world, secure a job wherever we lived, and raise my three children by myself for the past fifteen years. My Dutch stubbornness was rearing its head. If I had at least kept a journal of Dana's recurring, unfortunate, bad luck, "why does this have to happen to me?" experiences, I would have had a better understanding of the pattern that was evolving. I didn't see the need at the time.

By March Shanna reiterated her concerns about me paying her brother's bills and encouraged me to have him file for bankruptcy. With the ever-increasing bad economy, people were already beginning to lose their homes to banks. She pointed out that he didn't have any assets for them to take and with his current credit score he may as well be bankrupt. Well, we didn't follow that path. I was more concerned at the time about getting him healthy as his pains kept reoccurring. Finally the doctor suggested I take him to the esteemed Memorial Sloan Kettering Cancer Center in New York, so we scheduled an appointment and I drove him into the city the following Monday afternoon for more tests. They found nothing conclusive. The doctors there then suggested I take him to the Sloan facility in Basking Ridge for more tests that Thursday, which I did. No one could find anything wrong. I started to wonder what in hell was going on.

By midsummer his pain had increased and one day I was phoned by his employer saying that he had gone to the ER. I drove over to the hospital and immediately reached out to the doctor who had given me advice years earlier when Shanna had her seizure. After Dana summarized his symptoms and where he had recently been given tests, this doctor decided to operate. I suspect it was exploratory, because when he finally finished the procedure he came out and told me he had taken out Dana's appendix, but as far as he could see that wasn't the cause of the pain. He couldn't find the source of the problem. Dana was kept a few days and sent home, and the medical bills kept adding up. I wrote checks for a few more thousand dollars. Dana likely found his own method of dealing with the pain.

The New Year arrived and life was much the same. Dana continued at the restaurant and I continued trying to make some money in real estate. This was proving more and more difficult because, as in all parts of the country, our market had taken a downturn. I had already had to tap into my savings to keep on top of things. I was desperate for listings, anything I thought might sell. I called upon some folks whose listing had expired with another agent. After a few preliminary meetings with them, they decided they would list with me. I knew after just a week it was a bad decision. Times were difficult, but I had just signed up for what would become my biggest nightmare in real estate.

These clients were difficult and unrealistic. I was to accompany every showing with ample notice to them. OK, no big deal. The home was anything but warm and inviting. To make matters worse, they kept the heat at fifty degrees and required all prospective buyers to remove their shoes. They also wanted a Friday report each week bringing them up to date on the week's potential competitive properties and those which had sold. I complied with every one of their requests. I even gave them coffee and sat for several hours at a time with them when they would arrive unannounced in my office. I suspect they were looking for a warm place to go. I met potential buyers at their home (while they would lurk around the corner in their car and watch) and even shoveled their snow at times. They were wearing me down on a daily basis. This was only one listing in a very difficult market. The email they sent me when I suggested a price reduction to be more competitive in the market showed just how desperate I must have been to even decide to work with this couple. Desperate times, desperate measures and all that.

• • •

Linda, We TOTALLY disagree with your 'realtor explanation' on why no one has looked at our home in the past week or so. Maybe we can get together so we can explain to YOU how the manipulative verbiage of all you real estate agents is just why you all have such a bad rap in the community. Your goal is to FIRST get listings so you listing agents can sit back on your asses and HOPE another one from your tribe brings a buyer along AND to 'UNLOAD' homes

at the lowest prices you can to collect commissions
too quickly because you are all out there like hawks
trying anything in your power to land a sale because
so few homes are actually moving.

. . .

Lovely clients! As much as I would have benefited financially had
the home sold, I decided I had enough aggravation in my life without
compounding it with these two lunatics. I refused to work with them
any longer, which turned out to be a good decision on my part; sixteen
years later, the home had still not sold, despite a dozen different listing
agents. This wasn't my only listing at the time. I did have a "new build"
which actually wasn't built at all but just a hole in the ground. That
client couldn't bring himself to move forward as the economy was so
uncertain. Nothing was earning me money. Being a real estate agent
in 2010 was challenging and demanded all my attention. I knew I had
to do something if I was going to make it financially.

Then there were the home challenges. Since Dana was living at
home, even at the age of twenty-nine, he wanted to make his room
more inviting and comfortable if he had friends over. He got this grand
idea to buy a large sofa on eBay. Having finally located one, he set off
with a friend to pick it up. When they arrived home I asked him how
he was going to get it upstairs. His room was over the garage and
the staircase turned at a 90-degree angle. They tried. Shockingly, it
wouldn't fit through. Plan B was to take it upstairs and enter through
the door which abutted another bedroom. I told him that he should
measure the door first as it wasn't very wide. The next thing I knew,
he was removing the trim around the door so this bloody sofa would
fit through. He was so determined to make this work that he actually
cut off one end of the sofa with a hacksaw. Eventually he achieved his
goal, but my poor door was ruined. He promised me he would fix it.
No, that didn't happen. It was at least two years before I finally repaired
it myself. My home, as well as my bank account, was taking a beating.

It was about this time that the building phase really kicked in. Dana decided that he would like to try his hand at carpentry. At the time I thought it was a reasonable idea. In the hours he was home and not working at the restaurant, it would give him something to work on and a chance to perhaps improve his woodworking skills. He decided to make a table, a very large table. It was to be pieced together in individual sections by glue and then nails. I reached out to my brother Jim and told him what Dana wanted to do and he lent him an electric hand saw. Stressing the importance of safety, he loaned it to Dana. This project took on a life of its own. Dana made numerous trips to the hardware store and the next thing I knew, my garage had turned into a totally chaotic workshop. The sounds of sawing, sanding, hammering, and nailing were constant. He was enthusiastic, which I thought was commendable at the time. Then he started working on this thing for hours late into the night. When I asked him about that he told me he couldn't sleep, so decided to stay up and work. He spent hours—both day and night—in the garage, which by now looked like a bomb had recently exploded. Every inch of the garage was covered with what looked like two inches of sawdust. I was assured that he would clean the whole thing up just as soon as he reached the end of the nailing phase.

Despite the chaos, I wasn't too concerned. I knew Dana was busy. He was working long hours and also volunteering as an EMT in town. His schedule allowed him to do two or three shifts a week there. I was pleased he had found something worthwhile to do and felt at least he was finally headed in the right direction by being creative. The table progressed and so did the summer.

In late October Joe and I decided to book a trip to St. John in the Caribbean. Again, I felt Dana was well enough on his own; he wasn't a kid and he would manage just fine without us for a week. After a week of golf, sailing, and unexpectedly meeting up with old friends, we returned home. Dana greeted us at the door with an odd expression on his face.

"How did everything go while we were gone?' I asked sensing there was something he wanted to tell me.

"Great, Mom! But I have kind of a surprise for you. It isn't finished yet but I hope you like what I am doing."

By then I was in the house. I looked around my living room and saw that it was in complete disarray with the furniture from my office haphazardly placed in it.

"What the—" I started to ask him.

"Mom! I wanted to surprise you but I didn't finish yet. You know the paneling in your office? I decided it would look better painted so I have been trying to fill in all the gaps before painting it."

As I looked around all I could see were my dolls. I have lots of dolls, a very extensive collection from all my travels and an antique collection of Japanese dolls given to me as a gift. They were everywhere as they had been in the cabinets in my office. The furniture had all been removed and my files were everywhere. I took a deep breath,

"Dana. I know you are trying to help but you really should have asked me first. My collection is everywhere! And how I supposed to work in there?" I was trying not to get angry because I knew he had the best of intentions.

"OK, Mom, I'm sorry I didn't ask you but I just thought it would look better. You'll see when I'm finished."

I wasn't so sure but he had already started so now I had no choice but to let him carry out his plan, which took two more weeks to complete. This wasn't the first time he had decided to tackle a project while I was away to "help." The first time he had decided to paint all the grout in my kitchen tiles. Recalling these incidents, I confess that again, I failed to recognize the bizarreness of his behaviors.

If I knew anything by that point in my life, I did know to expect the unexpected. One of Dana's friends called it "Dana World." It wasn't always good news. And it usually involved Mom getting involved. A few weeks later I was awakened by Joe, who came in and told me I had an urgent phone call. I rolled over and looked at the clock to see it was 1 a.m. I knew it couldn't be a business call. I had always told my clients and customers that after 10 p.m. I was done for the day, unless we were negotiating, which for some reason frequently went on until close to midnight. I took the call to discover it was Dana.

"Mom, you need to come down here and help me! The police stopped me and they are arresting me! I haven't done anything wrong, I swear!"

After asking where he was, I threw on some clothes, jumped in my car, and headed over to the next town where he had been stopped. I was shocked to find not one, but three police cruisers at the scene.

Now this is a little overkill, I thought. There was no evidence of any accident, any damaged car, or anyone else involved. Dana sat in his car and looked terrified. He told me they had pulled him over because he had crossed a yellow line before turning into one of the local pubs. He swore he had done nothing wrong. Apparently, the police thought he had, because they arrested him and took him to the local jail. I followed. After I posted bail, they let him go. Fortunately, I had some friends on the force, although he did have to go to court. He had been driving without a license or registration and claimed he had forgotten to renew them. I paid the court fees, but fortunately did get reimbursed the bail money, which was almost $1,000. Like the one before, 2010 wasn't a great year either. As it turns out, though, it was better than what was to follow.

CHAPTER 12

THE DINNER

DANA WORKED EVERY restaurant shift that was offered to him over the holiday season. It was a "go to" place in town for special dinners and lunches. I would often encounter friends in town who had eaten there. They would comment to me that Dana had done a great job serving them and was so pleasant and friendly to everyone at their table. What mom doesn't want to hear this? While I was still trying to come to grips with the fact that he hadn't found a position in the business world, I thought maybe he had at least found some sort of niche for himself in the restaurant industry. He had recently been promoted and was now making decent money, and he had made many friends there. The table project, however, was still not completed. It was still very much under construction. I had not had use of my garage all winter.

On March 7, 2011, Shanna and Mike were coming over to dinner. I had invited them on a Monday because I liked to cook a nice dinner on nights when Dana did not have to work. He had worked all weekend at the restaurant and I thought it would be great to have everyone together that evening. This was something I did often. Shanna and Mike only lived in the next town and we frequently planned and executed meals together.

When they arrived around 5:30 p.m., Dana was not yet home. I was preparing one of their favorite meals—a nice roast of beef, twice-baked potatoes, and asparagus. Mike asked if there was anything he could do to help.

"Yes," I replied. "Could you please run down to the liquor store and pick up some wine? I totally forgot it and I only have white. It would be great to have some red to go with the meal."

I then asked Mike to wait a second so I could give him some cash. As I didn't have any in my wallet, I ran upstairs to the bedroom. In my bureau I kept a small purse to which I had been trying to add some cash every month to save up for a trip to Italy I was planning with my friends. When I opened the purse, though, there was no cash in it.

That's weird, I thought. *Maybe I put it somewhere else.* I called downstairs to Joe. "Hey, Joe, did you take any cash from my bureau?"

"Of course not," he answered. "I didn't even know you had any there. And besides, I would never take anything from there."

Okay, I thought. *It must be in some other place.* I proceeded to check out some small boxes in my jewelry cabinet. When I opened the blue satin box and saw it was empty, my heart stopped. This is where I kept a very special bracelet I had made for me in Thailand in 1970. I frantically looked through other boxes and noticed they were empty as well. Something was very wrong. It was clear I had been robbed.

My mind was a jumble. I couldn't think how this could have happened. I ran downstairs and told Joe that not only was my money gone, but a lot of my jewelry as well. He tried to calm me down, as did Mike and Shanna. The first thing I thought of was that the jewelry was insured, insured but irreplaceable. All of it had been specially made for me in either Bangkok or Brazil. Some I had purchased in Hong Kong. I knew I would not likely visit these places again and I was sick to my stomach.

"I can't believe this. I've been robbed," I said.

"What was taken?" Mike asked.

"About seven hundred dollars I was saving for my trip to Italy, and my gold bracelet. A lot of my other boxes are empty, but I'm not exactly sure until I take an inventory. I'm going to have to do that. And I'm going to need to contact the insurance company and the police."

Then Dana walked in the door and heard me talking to Mike.

"Mom, don't call the police," he said. He seemed agitated.

"Why not? My money is gone and so is my jewelry."

"I think I know who took it," he said.

"Well, who?" I yelled at him.

"There's this girl I have been hanging out with. She's been over here a few times and I think it was her."

"Well, you'd better go get her right now," I yelled at him, "or I am going to call the police."

He left immediately and I just looked at Mike, Shanna, and Joe.

"There's something strange going on here," Mike said. "Something is not right."

Dana returned about a half-hour later without the alleged girl. He went in the other room to talk to Mike, as I tried to get dinner organized in spite of what was going on. If I didn't, it was going to be ruined. When I finally got everything together and we all sat down, Dana began eating quietly. I could sense something was up but decided to wait until we had at least eaten. That was the quietest meal we ever had together.

When Dana took his last bite, I looked over at him and said, "Well, Dana, did you find her and speak to her?"

He looked at me and sobbed. "Mom, my friend didn't take your stuff. It was me. I took your stuff. I'm so sorry." Then he sadly looked at me and said, "I need help."

He confessed that he had taken the money to buy more of his drug. He was addicted to it and he really needed to get his life sorted out. I just sat there stunned. I didn't know what to say.

Then I blurted out, "And my bracelet! Where is my bracelet?"

"I sold it Mom. I'm sorry."

I felt sicker. I just slumped over and sat there staring at him. Looking back, I shouldn't have been surprised. I should have seen it coming, but I didn't. I didn't know he was an addict. I realized then that we were going to have to find a place to send him. I then took a deep breath and said, "Dana, we are going to get the help you need but right now you have to acknowledge that you need to get clean. And then we are going to find any and all drugs in your room." He agreed and went upstairs where I believe he phoned one of his friends.

The rest of that evening was a blur. My world was shattered. I had thought that I was an educated adult. I had had many life experiences. I had traveled to several countries, learned about varied cultures, saw that my children were educated and had managed a successful career for many years. This was an experience I had never encountered. I was about to enter a whole life I knew nothing about. I had no experience being the mother of a drug addict. I didn't know where to start. I didn't even know anyone who had experience in what I was about to encounter. I was really flying solo on this one.

The next day, while Dana spent the day sleeping on the sofa, I started doing what I had to do. Mike had suggested I call Dana's employment and tell them that he wouldn't be in for a while. I spoke with the HR department and they told me it wouldn't be a problem. Somewhat surprisingly, I was told Dana could go for treatment and return to work when he was deemed ready.

Then the bigger question had to be addressed of where to send him. The in-town facility was a possibility but not realistic, as it would make it too easy for him to just leave there and decide to come home. Something more removed was definitely the better choice. Hours and hours later, a short list was finally compiled. Then the phone calls began. I was new at this and didn't realize that, first of all, a space had to be available in the facility. It seemed that day I answered a million questions. Then there was the matter of insurance. Who was going to pay for this extended stay, which I knew was not inexpensive? I made more phone calls, consulting my daughters several times. I never even considered not helping him. On the path he was, I knew if he didn't get help, the next place I could most likely see him was in a jail cell dressed in an orange jump suit.

By late that evening we finally had a plan. A facility in Pennsylvania was our destination. When I told Dana about it, he was submissive and just looked at me blankly. Because he was experiencing total withdrawal from the drug, all he could do was sleep. I told him we were taking him the next morning to a facility to help him. I think he was expecting one of those fancy resort-type facilities as advertised on TV. I assured him it was not. Half-awake, he made his way to his room to pack.

I was mentally and physically exhausted. I had spent the entire day on the phone with counselors and the family to determine the next course of action. Julina and her husband Doug had decided to drive down from New York so that she could accompany me for the drive down to Philadelphia. We also decided that Shanna would come with us and that Doug and Mike would stay home and try and make sense out of Dana's room, which was by now a total disaster.

Before we would leave, though, I had some unfinished business. Feeling the need to at least try, I decided that if I could by some possible miracle locate my missing bracelet, I was going to make the effort. I asked Dana if he had gotten a receipt from the people he had sold it to. He had. In every town it seems there is some seedy area that touts "Gold Bought Here." I raced down to Route 22, a road I loathed and detested, and there I saw the place where he had pawned my precious bracelet. I made my way in and explained to the owner there had been a mistake and I wished to get it back.

He looked at me oddly and then said, "No, it isn't here anymore."

My heart lurched. I sobbed as I shakily walked back to my car. I knew I would never see it again. I realized at that point the depths Dana had sunken to in selling it. He knew that bracelet meant the world to me. I drove home gripping the steering wheel, so furious I couldn't see straight. The total outlandishness of his actions made me realize we had to get the best help we could find for him. He had to get better and I had to move on.

Doug and Julina arrived early the next morning, as did Shanna and Mike. Dana was still sleeping when I went to get him, and he hadn't packed yet. I read off a list of what he could and couldn't bring and helped him sort out his stuff. He was still in a stupor and hadn't eaten much in the past twenty-four hours.

Eventually we collected everything we thought he needed and set out on the most depressing road trip I have ever taken. Dana slept in the back seat as the girls and I discussed what lay ahead.

Finally Julina said, "Let's just hope he's not with us on the ride home."

In my angst and uncertainty, I seriously hadn't considered the fact that, after all of this, the facility may not accept him. I didn't even want to think about what that would mean. What if I had to return home with him? Then what would I do? My girls kept encouraging me to be positive. I was so glad to have them with me because I don't think I could have done that trip on my own.

As we neared the facility, Dana finally woke up announcing he was hungry and wanted a strawberry milkshake. We all just looked at each other. We needed a break anyway, so I thought, *Why not?* It would be the last thing we could do for him for a while. We found a Dairy Queen and he managed to make his way inside. He returned to the car with his milkshake and asked where we were. When I told him we were ten minutes away from our destination, he looked around and I could tell it wasn't exactly what he had expected. We were now in a rather questionable neighborhood in the outskirts of Philadelphia.

Fortunately, when we arrived at the facility we noted that it was located in a somewhat better neighborhood. At least this place had trees and some outdoor space. Well, it would have to do. We were met by a rather surly receptionist, which wasn't what I was expecting either. Apparently, she had seen a lot of "intakes" and this was nothing new to her. To me it was. I was out of my element here and so were my daughters. They should have been at work and so should I. We shouldn't have been there trying to get my son admitted to rehab, but there we were. She handed us each a form to fill out and told us to each do it separately and not discuss what we were writing among ourselves. We proceeded to do as she asked. Meanwhile, someone came in to take Dana into another room, presumably to interview him. I wasn't sure how capable he was of conducting a conversation at this point. As he stood up to follow her, all I could see was how rail thin he was, with sunken eyes and a totally unkempt appearance. As I gazed at him I felt nothing but total sadness. This was without a doubt the most depressing moment of my life. All I could think of was that somehow I had totally let him down.

The girls and I continued filling out our questionnaires. Mostly they wanted history on his recent communicative skills, hygiene, sleeping habits, appetite, and irritability. Apparently, we answered all the questions to their satisfaction. After two hours of waiting and hoping we were finally given the word. They would accept him. We all breathed a huge sigh of relief. Someone else was going to help him this time. Mom hadn't done such a good job apparently.

We were then informed about the family services offered to us. They wanted us to be part of the process. They explained that addiction is a "family disease" and, while it's the individual who has the symptoms, behavior, and consequences, the loved ones are caught up in these difficult times. Their experience, they said, is that a person has a much greater chance of success in treatment–and after—when his or her loved ones are part of the process. They also told us that family members and caring friends often feel powerless to stop the addict from the downward spiral. Our begging, pleading, bargaining, and threats are all useless in our attempts to prevent the addict from self-destruction. They explained that it's difficult to understand how a person who loves us (and whom we love) can continue to hurt us so much. Moreover, they went on to say that many times we feel responsible for their abuse.

Well what a novel thought, I said to myself. *I certainly do.*

Their program was to start with a "Day of Enlightenment," described as a "new beginning" for families. My heart was already beginning to feel a bit lighter. We would learn how to deal with the many conflicting emotions that another person's addiction can generate, and how to examine our own lives in relation to the addicted person to give us new perspectives and ideas. The program was required to have visitation rights to the patient. I had no problem with that and was looking forward to participating. Not only did I want to help Dana, but we were also told the program would teach us:

- We are not at fault
- We can acquire the tools and understanding necessary to protect ourselves from possible future emotional hurt
- We could begin to grow as a family again, no matter what the addict in our life may do

The sessions were to be offered there on the site. I signed up for the first one, which would take place the following Saturday. My daughters also wanted to attend, but Julina was pregnant. The seven-hour round trip would be a lot for her. Shanna wanted to attend, but she already had a commitment that day with Mike. The girls had already taken time off from work for the two-hour drive down. It was decided I would bring Joe, as he was now again living in my home and was around Dana the most. We would start with that. At this point in his life, Dana did not have a girlfriend or significant other. No surprise there. He was a bit of a mess. Our intent was to share with everyone what we learned at the sessions.

I was overwrought with emotions as we left the facility. I could not believe I had just put my son into rehab, but the reality was starting to set in. Major changes would have to be made, not only in his life but in mine, as well.

My daughters hugged me as I cried and said, "Mom, it's going to be OK now. He's where he needs to be."

I nodded mutely and climbed in the car. On the drive back we discussed what we had written on the questionnaires given to us. It was amazing how we had all answered the questions almost identically. We all had stressed how his dress and personal hygiene had totally deteriorated. He was certainly not the same young man he once was.

In their attempt to lighten the moment, my girls then went on to remind me of some of the incidents that had occurred previously. Some I had forgotten about, or maybe I just wanted to. No car was safe with Dana it seemed. While Joe and I had been on a trip the previous year, Dana had borrowed my car to go to the hardware store. He called me while we were away and told me he had been in a slight accident with my car. Apparently, he hadn't stopped in time at the intersection at the end of our street and rammed another car. The "slight" accident cost me nearly $4,000 in repairs. And he got a ticket again. It seriously reached the point that whenever Dana's name appeared on the screen of my phone I had to brace myself for whatever bad news was to follow.

When the next incident had occurred, there was no phone call. It was a surprise. Later that year Joe and I had traveled up to Vermont to visit my brother. We had taken my car and left Joe's Mercedes in the driveway. When we returned Joe went out to his car for something and saw the front bumper was askew. He shook it to see what was going on and it fell off the car to the ground. Clearly it had been damaged. When Joe questioned Dana about this later, he confessed that he needed to back it out of the driveway to get something into the garage (for his table project), and in doing so had hit the culvert with the bumper. He didn't want to tell Joe, so he tried to put it back on with duct tape. Like this wasn't going to be noticed. I had told him many times almost anything could be fixed with duct tape, but he had taken it to a whole new level.

Oh Dana! Hopefully now, with help, these crazy incidents will end, I thought.

When we finally returned to my house from the rehab facility late that afternoon, we found that Doug and Mike had been hard at work. They had taken it upon themselves to start sorting out Dana's room. First, they handed me a huge box of unopened mail. Then they told me they had been through every drawer, every cabinet, every article of clothing, and any other possible hiding places for drugs. Their attempts were not unrewarded and they handed me some fifteen different prescription vials, all from different doctors. I wasn't even sure what some of them were. They had also uncovered what seemed to be a hideout for smoking lord-knows-what in the large eave adjacent to his room. It had been furnished with easy chairs for added comfort. We all conjectured about what had taken place there. The room itself was a total disaster. One look told me this was going to be another major project, but my sons-in-law offered to help. After I told them about the Saturday family session offered by the rehab facility, they offered to come back then and tackle the room. I gratefully accepted their offer.

The laundry list of jobs facing me the next day seemed daunting. After speaking again with the HR rep at Dana's employer, I then had to check on his disability insurance. Hours were spent trying to figure out who was going to pay for the rehab and how. Dana's cell phone had to be canceled and, as he wasn't going to be driving for some time, I also had to cancel his auto insurance. I needed to phone family members as well, to fill them in on the situation. After one call I decided to send an email to my brothers telling them what had happened, because I realized I was still so emotional I couldn't relate the story without breaking into tears.

Once all the necessary calls and emails were finished, I decided to look at the pill vials to try and make some sense out of them. The number and variety of prescriptions came as a shock to me. I had thought it was only Adderall he was taking. I had a lot to learn. I knew calling the doctors would be of no help, as privacy laws would prevent them from telling me anything, so I started researching some of the prescriptions myself. It was then I realized how much I had missed. Here was my son living under my same roof for the past fifteen months, and I had failed to see that he was taking all these drugs. Where the hell had I been during all of this? I knew I had been busy working, but was that any excuse to have missed all the signs which were obviously in front of me the whole time? I became even more depressed. I knew I needed to go to one of those sessions because now I was partially blaming myself.

After taking a mental break, I next tackled the box of unopened mail. Being from New Jersey, I had several expletives in my repertoire to express my reaction to what I found. There were piles and piles of unopened bills, notices of late payments, letters from collection agencies, and, what do you know, his passport which had "never arrived." Evidently, he hadn't found any need to open his mail for God knows how long.

I spent the next two days opening mail, making lists, and calling places he owed money. When they said they couldn't talk to me, I explained if they ever hoped to see a dime they best talk to me, because the debtor had nothing and they would have better luck getting blood from a stone. It didn't matter. So I compiled lists, lots of lists. And I wrote checks, lots of checks to at least make a dent in some of the balances he had accrued. He owed physicians, dentists, hospitals, outpatient centers, the DMV, the municipal court, and several collection agencies. This was to be a long day, as was the next, when I did pretty much the same thing. It was mentally exhausting. I decided then and there I was going to get a Power of Attorney so I would no longer be in the dark about Dana's affairs. I knew this would be time-consuming and costly, but I felt it was worth it. I was also going to have to get Dana's approval on it. We would address that later. Spending so much time on his financial matters was preventing me from doing my real estate work. After attempting to make some necessary calls and falling short of sounding positive and enthusiastic, I realized that was going to have to be put on hold until the following week. My anxiety level was rising.

On Saturday, my sons-in-law arrived early at my house to perform an overhaul on Dana's room while Joe and I set out to visit him at rehab. I expected this was to be the second of many drives I would make down to Philadelphia. When we arrived, it was explained that there would be no visiting with the patient until we had completed at least the first six-hour course with the counseling staff. When we entered the "family session", I looked around the room to check out what other unfortunate souls were experiencing this nightmare. It was not an enthusiastic group. We were all sullen, unhappy, and pretty much all pissed off. A few of us spoke before the meeting, and I discovered one family was there the fourth time for their daughter. Holy shit, how was that even possible? I figured she must be addicted to hard drugs like heroin. At least Dana was only taking prescription drugs. Naïve? Yep.

The counselor began the meeting by having us all go up to a very large chalkboard in the room to write down adjectives describing how we were feeling. Every word imaginable was written, including angry, disappointed, hurt, frustrated, distressed, annoyed, irate, deceived, and most of all, broke. The process had the desired effect. It made us feel that we were all experiencing the exact same emotions. It demonstrated that we were all in the same boat, regardless of each family member's specific addiction. It was a good start.

I learned in the next hour that I was guilty of doing nearly all the things on their not-to-do list, including cleaning up his messes, bailing him out of jail, paying bills I was not responsible for, and doing his laundry. I had a lot to learn. The intent of the meeting was to teach the families how to change enabling behaviors. We were taught DOs, DONTs, and effective communication methods. We were also versed on chemical dependency and brain chemistry. This is when I learned about dopamine and the effects it has on the brain. We were given lists of medications to be avoided and lists of services available to families. In short, it was a crash course on how to deal with an addict in your family. This was a course I had never taken and one I wouldn't wish on anyone else. It was exhausting, but afterwards we were allowed to see Dana.

At least he looked clean and better kept than when we had last seen him. We hugged and he told me how sorry he was that he was there and had put me through this. I told him I loved him and just wanted him to get better. He asked about his sisters and I told him they all sent their love and wanted him to get clean. We only had about twenty minutes together as he had to attend a scheduled meeting. I assured him I had completed the six-hour course to be able to visit him and would be back the following week.

The following day, Sunday, I remember going to church, where I saw friends greeting one another and laughing together. I sensed calmness in them that I didn't feel in myself. I felt I was the only one with this huge burden and I didn't know how to react or interact with the people around me. I felt isolated and alone. I was sure that several people had heard where Dana was and that I was being judged. I prayed a lot that day. After the service I had a chance to speak with the pastor and that helped, but I knew that the days, weeks, and months ahead were going to be filled with feelings of guilt and unanswered questions. Hoping the sessions that were offered at the center would be helpful, I knew all I could do was go about my daily routine and try to reconstruct some sort of normalcy to my life. I was deeply hurting though, and it became easier to avoid friends than to speak with them.

CHAPTER 13

TURNING THE CORNER

THE FOLLOWING SATURDAY I drove down alone to visit with Dana. Joe couldn't make it as he had clients he had to meet that day. I wasn't going to push it, as he wasn't Dana's father. At least he had gone through the basic course with me the previous week to get a handle on how to cope living with a recovering addict. It was then I realized I could use the term "recovering." Progress was being made.

And speaking of the father, you may have wondered at this point where Dylan was in all of this. I received an email from him right after Dana entered the rehab facility. The email said that Dana had called him. It was the first time they had spoken in two years and they only spoke briefly, but Dylan had told Dana he was rooting for him. Great! Dylan was rooting, and I was doing all the hard work. This parent wasn't getting much in the way of help from the other parent. Not that I expected it. I didn't ask Dylan for help, figuring he hadn't been around anyway. It seemed family cohesiveness was not our strong suit.

When I arrived at the rehab facility that next week, I was met by the son I used to know. After just a week and a half of sufficient rest, a healthy diet, and—most importantly—no drugs, he looked like a different person. I knew he had a long way to go in his recovery, but this seemed like a good beginning. He first showed me his room and introduced me to his roommate. As we explored the facility, he pointed out different areas and talked about the various kinds of meetings he attended. We then decided to go for a walk.

The "campus" of the facility was nothing fancy. Comprised of various stone and wooden buildings surrounding a small lake, it was rather peaceful. As we headed toward the lake, Dana explained that the staff encouraged exercise and outdoor activities in addition to attending all the mandatory meetings. I didn't press him for details about how he thought he had ended up there. That discussion could wait for a later time. I wanted him to focus on the positive achievements he was now making as opposed to how screwed up his life had been before. I was trying to provide positive reinforcement and offer encouraging feedback. The burning question I wanted to ask him was how he had ended up with so many prescriptions. There was a nagging feeling in my mind that it would be a long time before I discovered the answer.

During that afternoon lake walk, Dana expressed to me his desire to pursue a different career path. He wanted to do something worthwhile to help people. He told me he had been thinking a lot about it while there and thought he might like to try and become a nurse or a counselor. This surprised me a bit as he had always been rather squeamish around blood and the like, but I told him if that's what he wanted we could discuss it further. I also pointed out that it was going to require another degree. He said he knew that, but perhaps some of his college credits could apply toward obtaining a nursing degree. I believe he was quite impressed with the staff at the facility and this had a major impact on his decision-making process. While I wasn't sure the idea was totally realistic, I encouraged him to think about it more and we would discuss it the next time I visited.

I left there that afternoon feeling much better than I had in a very long time. My son was getting the help he needed. I felt we were on our way to hopefully arriving at the end of a very long and arduous journey. I hoped that he could stay for an extended period of time to enable him to recover sufficiently both mentally and physically.

Unfortunately, this was not to be. In their infinite wisdom the insurance company determined that it would only cover his stay through March 16. He had only been there eleven days. I'm no doctor, but I knew this was simply not enough time. The facility called me on the 15th and said the insurance company would not pay anymore. I told them that was ridiculous, which of course it was, but to no avail. I told them I couldn't go that very day and get him. It was late in the day and I was about two hours away—not considering traffic. Moreover, I wasn't sure I was mentally ready to take over the task of having him back in my house and overseeing the continuation of his recovery. This was all new to me.

At one of their family sessions, the facility had stressed the importance of having a "contract" with the addict, setting rules and boundaries that would have to be adhered to. I hadn't developed that contract yet. I needed at least a day to get my head around this and told them so. That was fine, they agreed, but it would cost $450 for that extra day. I paid it.

The following day I drove down to pick him up and take him home. The staff explained that he would need to start a forty-hour per week program near home. We discussed where this might take place and I mentioned a facility located in our town. We could look into that. I expressed my concern that he was being released too soon, but they again explained that the staff at the facility had not made the decision to send him home. They saw the benefit of keeping him, but it wasn't their decision. Not a great fan of insurance companies.

On the way home, Dana and I had time to discuss boundaries. I stressed to him that this was it. He needed to comply with every request and rule of the program so there would be no relapse. I told him how I had heard stories from others in the facility of how their kid had been there multiple times. I explained to him this was not going to happen to him, could not happen to him, and that I wasn't going be responsible for any recurring trips. He was in total agreement. He knew what he had to do and would do anything the family and the program requested of him. I explained to him that we were going to draw up the recommended contract when we got home.

He returned to his bedroom, now stripped of TV, comfy sofas, and pictures. It was now no frills. Doug and Mike had done a great job rehabbing it for him. There were no reminders of what had gone on there before, which is the way it should have been. Nevertheless, I did get an email from my ex saying that a clause in the contract should require Dana to "rehab the room himself." While I'm sure it might have been beneficial, it was also totally unrealistic. Considering the projects he had attempted in the past, it was unlikely that his new environs were going to be set up the way I felt they should be. As far as I was concerned, my sons-in-law had done an outstanding job.

Dana was not even two weeks clean. I hardly considered that out of the woods. Perhaps had he been able to stay longer at the facility I might have felt differently. Because I was new at this and realized his wellbeing was totally in my hands, I decided I had the final say. When I asked Dana what we should do about the unfinished table in the garage, he said, "Take it to the dump." I considered this a good step in moving forward and agreed.

We finally hashed out The Contract, which covered controlling his finances, drug testing, rules of the house, attendance of meetings, television time, eating habits, etc. Dana agreed to everything and signed it. In his ensuing discussion with his dad, Dana told him he recognized that he needed to depend on firm rules and guidelines to provide an essential safety net to maximize the odds for his recovery. He appeared to be clearheaded and cognizant, but as a recovering addict he still had a long road ahead of him. He was going to need a lot of guidance.

Fortunately, our town had a center for people needing help on their way to recovery. Meetings were held there on a consistent basis, and Dana soon became a regular. I accompanied him to some as well to try and get a better handle on the situation. By this time he seemed accustomed to sitting in the circle of people discussing his problems, life, and addiction. I was not. I just listened. It was clear to me that some of the people there were veterans of this. I could only hope that this was the beginning of the end of a long nightmare, and the meetings and his resilience would see him through this.

After a week, I broached the subject of the power of attorney letter. Once I explained to him that this would enable me to speak with any and all doctors and anyone connected to his finances, he realized the benefit of it. He agreed to sign it knowing I had his best interests in mind. That was one of the smartest decisions I made in the entire course of mayhem that had occurred and what was to ensue. It was in large part because of this POA that I was able to finally determine how Dana had managed to get so many prescriptions. Not being familiar with the term "doctor shopping," I had a lot to learn and I did. I soon became aware of what had transpired.

After a lot of questioning and investigation I came to realize that Dana, like so many others, had his prescription filled by many different doctors. It's a known fact that addicts lie to their doctors. Dana apparently was good at this because not one of the dozen doctors who were prescribing him medication had cause to know that he was having prescriptions filled by eleven others. How is it that our society manages to track nearly every aspect of our lives— credit, insurance claims, social security, mortgages, health insurance, child molesters, and even our Amazon searches—yet somehow no one has come up with an effective system for doctors to alert them that an addict has just had a prescription refilled or filled for the first time by multiple physicians? Is that so hard? This is a national problem, so why isn't someone doing something about it? Millions of young adults abuse the system and, as a result, become addicted to prescription drugs. Some are not so lucky.

Shortly after Dana returned home, we received news that one of his friends had died. The young man had also grown up in Summit in an affluent family and had once been on Dana's hockey team. After college he had moved to California. Cause of death: drug overdose. I was shaken to the core. This insidious disease does not discriminate. This could have been Dana. We were lucky. He had gone to rehab and was now clean. I couldn't comprehend the grief that this other family must have been experiencing. I became even more determined that would not happen in my family, no matter what I had to do. Realizing that I had power of attorney, I proceeded to seek out doctors to chastise, the ones who had filled his prescriptions. Once they realized I had this POA, they knew they had to take my unfriendly calls. Hopefully I ruined their day.

By the beginning of April, Dana was able to return to his job at the restaurant. Prior to his doing so he did a lot of research on nursing schools nearby that he might attend. We discussed this at length and I agreed it could be a great start to a new beginning. It was finally decided that he should start courses at the community college, which was about a half-hour away. This plan seemed viable because he could work in the restaurant during the day and go to school at night. Before that could commence, however, he had another priority, his teeth.

Like any other facet of his drug abuse, I was totally unaware of how the use of drugs affects the teeth. I was floored when he returned from his dentist and announced he had to have tooth extractions, a root canal, and that he had gum disease. Unbeknownst to me but apparently a well-known fact, drugs reduce the flow of saliva and cause dry mouth. Dry mouth in turn significantly increases the risk of tooth decay because the saliva reduces the bacteria in the mouth. Because he had been taking and abusing drugs since 2005, some six years, the amount of tooth damage was significant. The work had to be done. There was no getting around it or postponing it. He scheduled the appointments to have several teeth removed.

The year 2011 did a number on my bank account. Some $2,000 was paid to the dentist. The doctor and hospital bills kept pouring in.

Then there was the matter of tuition for nursing school. I paid that as well. When I totaled the money I spent that year alone, sorting out his debts and problems, I was aghast, but I didn't see a way around it. I decided that I would draw up a loan agreement between Dana and myself and he could pay me back later. I explained to him it was a loan and not a gift. We sorted out the terms and drew up the paperwork. I still wasn't convinced that Dana filing bankruptcy was the best option. Because I now had power of attorney, I was able to speak with creditors and was able to do some negotiating with them.

By August of that year Dana started his nursing school program. Fortunately, some of his college credits were accepted, but not as many as we had hoped. But it was a start. He attended his classes, worked at the restaurant, went to his meetings, and stayed clean. I was constantly monitoring to see that all this happened without trying to be a helicopter mom. He was an adult, now twenty-nine years old, but really bad things had happened and I was determined that there were to be no repeats.

As if life were not challenging enough, 2011 saw Hurricane Irene slam our state and states nearby. Fortunately, we weren't in the beach area where so many people lost their homes, but it rained heavily. I was over at a neighbor's house for a party and, not realizing the extent of the rain until late that evening, I wasn't even thinking about possible damage. When I arrived home Dana told me he was going down to the basement to do some laundry. Halfway down the stairs he called up.

"Mom, you better come see this! The litter box is floating away!"

Not realizing what he was talking about, I ran to the basement door and started to descend the stairs.

"Oh, crap!"

Literally. The cat's litter box was floating in over two feet of water. This was not good. This was very, very bad. I knew that this was also terrible for my furnace (located in the flooded basement) and tried to think of what to do. Water and electricity do not make good bedfellows. After a few moments, I decided to call the fire department. I explained what was happening and they said they would be there shortly. Half an hour later they arrived and were able to pump out most of the water. When they left, I looked around the finished basement and realized that not only the carpet but the walls, cabinets, and contents of all the closets were in total ruin. Dana and I just looked around at the total mess and then at each other.

"Well, it looks like we have another project," I said, trying to remain calm. Knowing it was going to take a lot of money to repair all the damage, I grabbed my camera and started taking pictures.

"Why are you taking pictures of this?" he asked. My, he had a lot to learn.

"They're for the insurance company. They're going to want to see everything that is here, and everything that has been damaged." This was in fact the second time this had happened. Dana hadn't been home the first go-round. I already knew the drill. My newly finished basement was going to have to undergo yet another renovation. I was getting tired of surprises, especially the expensive ones.

After calling a company to dry out the basement, I hired another company for repairs. It was ready in time for the holidays. Life managed to go on without any other setbacks for the next several months. I continued trying to make a living, but the real estate market hadn't bounced back the way we had all hoped. I was still catching up on a lot of bills, tuition had to be paid, and so did the mortgage. I also wasn't getting the amount of rental income from my property in Hilton Head that I had anticipated. By the end of the year I realized I was in a rather dire situation if I didn't sell something quickly.

My hopes were based on a couple I had been driving around for what seemed like forever. They were trying to relocate from a nearby town and also had a home to sell. I kept thinking that if I could only pull this together everything would be OK financially. After days of bouncing from one home to the next, we walked into a property that I thought would work for them. We spent a good two hours there and they decided to make an offer. I told them I would go back to my office to write it up. On the drive back, I pulled over to the side of the road and stopped, weeping like a baby because I was so relieved. That's when I realized that I couldn't go on like that for much longer. I decided then and there that when those transactions came together I was going to have to think about an exit plan. I was worn out.

As the new year approached so did my anxiety. I knew I needed to sell my house. I already had a place in South Carolina, so why not just pack up and move there? Dana was doing well. He had been clean now for almost two years and was excelling in nursing school. He also was able to quit the restaurant job because he found employment working in the hospital emergency room. He didn't need me looking over his shoulder every day to monitor his life. In the evening I spent hours sitting outside on my patio looking at the stars, silently asking my dad for advice. Oddly, I heard his voice in my head saying, "Just sell the damn house!" I decided to do just that.

By spring the real estate market was beginning to look more promising. This was probably a good time to sell. I had been thinking of nothing else for the past several months, so I set about editing, painting, and staging the house. This consumed my life for several months, but I felt like I was working toward a better life. I really wanted to leave New Jersey, its high taxes, and the all-consuming job of real estate.

A few months into spring, having completed most of my to-do list, I first called my financial advisor to make sure this was a viable option. We had a long conversation but when all was said and done he assured me that I was making the right decision. This was great news! I was going to start to make my exit plan. But first, I needed to do something about the hall bathroom. Having successfully completed other home repair projects, I set out to make some tile repairs. I headed to Home Depot to get caulk, tiles, and glue and, feeling very good about myself, I stood in line to check out. Suddenly I felt a horrific pain in my chest. I gasped and bent over, dropping what I had on the floor. Someone asked if I was alright and I nodded yes, managed to walk outside, and leaned against the outside wall.

A few minutes later I was able to call Dana (who was still a volunteer EMT) on my cell phone and tell him what had happened. He asked me where I was and he called an ambulance, which arrived within minutes. By this time I was feeling better, but they wanted to check me out. They took my heart rate, which was quite high. After a bit they said I had had an anxiety attack and asked if anything unusual happened that day.

"Yep," I replied with a laugh. "My advisor told me I could retire. Do you think that's why I'm anxious?"

The culmination of all that had gone before had clearly led up to this. I wanted to go home, but the EMTs advised me to go to the hospital to be monitored for the rest of the day. So that's where I went. The bathroom project would have to wait.

The next day I returned home and called my repair person, Ritchie, to come and look at the bathroom. He was my go-to fix-it person for jobs for myself and my clients and I trusted him implicitly. He looked at the mess I had made and said that all the tiles should be taken out. Given that the house was built circa 1939, he suggested that a whole new bathroom be put in. Realizing it was the right thing to do but also knowing I didn't have extra money, I told him I couldn't. I explained I was trying to fix the house up to sell it.

No one does what Ritchie did next. He told me that he would do the work, and when the house sold I could pay him. He explained that he was so grateful I had given him so much work over the past several years he wanted to repay me. It was so generous on his part, but I couldn't let him do that. He needed the money even more than I did, so we decided to do a bathroom. We hopped in his truck, went to Home Depot (this time no panic attacks) and picked everything out together. He completed the project within a month and my home went on the market the next week. I hoped it would sell fast. The bills were quickly adding up.

All too aware that I was leaving Dana, and not knowing where he could go and live, this started to consume my thoughts as well.

Dana was thinking about it, too. He knew he was going to have to get a roommate as he couldn't afford the high rents of the Garden State by himself. He also had to stay in the county because the college he was attending was a county college. The tuition would have been at least double were he to move out of county. After several months we came up with a plan. He decided to room with one of his friends from the restaurant. They were going to rent my friend Maggie's house, as she was now going to be working in Philadelphia. It was a perfect solution. Knowing he was going to have a nice, safe place to live relieved me immensely.

What seemed liked hundreds of potential buyers traipsed through our home. After a few months of not receiving an offer, I realized the house itself was not the problem. It was the underground oil tank for our furnace that was deterring people. Though it was only nine years old, the media had done a wonderful job scaring people about these tanks with their possible leakage and the environmental consequences. Insurance was in place for the tank, but that didn't seem to be enough. So I hired a company to yank it out and then a new furnace had to be put in. Selling a home is such fun! Two weeks later we had a buyer. This was now moving very quickly, as we had to be out of the house by June.

May and June were a total blur. I had to sort through years of accumulated "stuff" and decide what I could live without. I joked to my friends that we spent our early years, first married, trying to accumulate all we could, and our later years trying to get rid of it all. Because I was going to move to my already-furnished condo in Hilton Head, whatever I took from New Jersey was going in storage. Dana was a great help in transferring large pieces of furniture to my daughter, which I figured she was getting anyway so why move them twice? We held sales and donated the leftovers, with Dana taking some items to his new digs. The movers arrived and, *voila,* it was over.

I had mixed feelings about the move. The stress of money and constant anxiety had led me to this decision, but I was leaving my son, my home, my job, my friends, and life as I knew it. I hoped I was making the right choice. I had a lot of time to think about it on the drive down I-95. The car was loaded to its capacity, complete with plants and a broom. I thought it rather comical as I noted all the last-minute junk I had thrown in the car. Now it was just me and the junk. I was anxious for the first hour, but then suddenly I felt like the world had been lifted from my shoulders and I sang along to country songs for the rest of the trip.

CHAPTER 14

LOTS OF CHANGES

WHILE DANA WAS making his own life in New Jersey in his new home, I was making my own in Hilton Head. Fortunately, Shanna and her husband were already living there with my granddaughter. I was looking forward to being near them and spending weekends on the beach. After a few months I decided I wanted to move to the north end of the island where they lived. The search began for a new home, but first I needed to sell my condo. Exhausted from recently selling the New Jersey home, I did not relish the thought. This one I couldn't list myself, as I still was working toward getting my South Carolina real estate license. This time I didn't have any major repairs to make, so it was relatively easy to prep it for selling.

I had bought the condo in 2005. It was now 2013 and the real estate market had not recovered fully in Hilton Head as it had in other areas. I resigned myself to the fact I was going to lose money. "Buy high, sell low" was not exactly what I had in mind, but I really wanted a house so I could get all my worldly possessions out of storage.

Even though I knew I would be losing money on the condo, I felt positivity in my life I hadn't felt in a long time. It was the first time in years I was not writing checks to cover Dana's expenses. He and his roommate kept pace with their obligations. Rent and utilities were paid on time. They had plenty of food. Dana had a decent paying job at the hospital and even had health insurance. These simple facts of life that other parents seemed to take for granted had finally become a way of life for my son. When it came time to pay the semester's tuition, he was for the first time, able to contribute. Life was looking brighter and I was so looking forward to enjoying it for a change. I put my condo on the market in December and waited for the perfect buyer.

When the Christmas season arrived, my friend Karen and I decided to take a road trip and drive back to New Jersey where her family lived as well. We had known each other for years before moving to Hilton Head. I wanted to visit Dana in his new environs and see for myself how everything was going. My other daughter was in New York with her family, so that would be the next stop. Karen and I set out at 4 a.m., the car stacked to the roof with Christmas presents for my family, her family, and what seemed like for the whole county. These two grannies laughed and giggled their way through South Carolina and North Carolina. Then we exited onto a four-lane road in Virginia to take a "shortcut." I was driving and told Karen we had better watch our speed because Virginia police have a nasty habit of nailing speeders on the side roads. No sooner than the words were out of my mouth we saw a patrol car pull a quick u-turn, hit his lights, and set out after us. I just looked at Karen. We were not laughing. He pulled us over and told me I was speeding.

"Officer," I said in my sweetest voice, "we just exited from I-95. I know the speed limit is different here, but I was trying to figure out how to get this damn car off cruise control. I can't figure out how to do this! We're just trying to get home for Christmas to see our kids. And, oh my God, you look so much like my son!!"

Karen was trying not to break up laughing. The young officer peered in the back and saw enough gifts to amply cover Christmas for multiple families. Then he asked where we were from. When we told him we had driven from Hilton Head he said, "Oh, I love it down there. I was just there with my uncle fishing. Great place!" He issued us a warning and showed me how to take the car off cruise control, which I already knew. Karen and I laughed all the way to New Jersey. We couldn't get it out of our head that if we somehow needed extra money for a ticket or something else for our trip, all we had to do was pull over and have a Christmas sale. My God, it felt so good to laugh again.

When I arrived at Dana's I was thrilled to see that they had set up house so well, had a well-stocked fridge and a routine that worked for everyone. He and his roommate were most accommodating. This was the first experience I had visiting Dana as an adult in his own place. We did normal things. We cooked dinner, sat around, laughed, and watched TV. By this time, he had also re-established a relationship with his sisters and brothers-in-law and was looking forward to spending time with his young nieces. After a few days in New Jersey, we all drove up to New York to spend Christmas together. I felt encouraged and relieved. Dana's life seemed finally on track.

After the holidays, I received an offer on my condo and set about finding a house. I had finally gotten my South Carolina real estate license so this simplified my search. I had been looking for almost a year, knew what I wanted and found the perfect home after just one day. *One last move*, I told myself. This would be move number twenty-four. (Coincidence? that was the house number.) I needed a place where I never had to leave. A place I could roll in and out of if need be. I was through with stairs. When I initially started looking it was in the back of my mind that the place would need a separate apartment for Dana should he need to come and stay with me. Now, that was no longer necessary. I brought Shanna and Mike through the house and they loved it, too. It was less than a mile from them. Perfect. I offered and by the next day I knew where I was going to spend the rest of my life. I closed in April 2014.

The story should have ended here. I was in my new home and Dana was finally on a good path. But unfortunately it was not over.

While I can't blame any one person, one's life is largely determined by external factors, perhaps the most important being the people with whom we surround ourselves. Such was to be in Dana's case.

During the next few months while I was busy moving (again) and getting settled into my new home, Dana was moving on with his own activities. His life was moving in the right direction. Not only was he working in the ER at the hospital in Summit and attending his nursing program, but he also was still working as an EMT in Summit. Through this job, and about at this time, he met a young woman who worked in the police department. They had cause to interact constantly because when the EMTs were called the police intervened as well. It was about midyear when the two of them began to date.

When Dana told me about her I was happy for him—happy that he was with a person who would and could love and accept him in spite of the many issues he had. After all, at just four years clean, he was still a recovering addict. He told me that his girlfriend was a caring and understanding person. She was single with a child, but her ex-husband was not around because of his own issues. The girlfriend, whose name was Lauren, lived with her sister in the adjacent town. I knew Dana was spending a lot of time with her. He told me that they had become close and he had formed a special relationship with her son.

Unfortunately, just when everything seemed to be going well on all fronts, he was faced with yet another challenge. My friend Maggie, whose house Dana was renting, informed him that she was going to have to move back into her house as her job was changing again. She also had a new boyfriend, and she wanted him to come and live with her. This was not news I wanted to hear, not about the boyfriend, but about the house. Now Dana was going to have to move again. He was going to have to find a place to live and be close enough to commute and still attend his nursing classes. He finally decided to move in with his friend Dan, whom he had met through his rehab sessions. It was someone he liked and respected. I was on board with this decision, knowing that his friend was totally in-the-know regarding Dana's past. Dan had at one point been Dana's mentor in the program. Dana made the move, even though it added forty-five minutes to his commute each way.

Dana's schedule became quite full as he was spending a lot of time with Lauren and her son Jayden while still working at the hospital and juggling his EMT schedule. With the longer commute to and from school, he confessed he was usually tired but happy. His days were jam packed but we managed to speak often. I did not see him again until the following Christmas because of his busy schedule.

That Christmas, we all convened at Julina's and Doug's home in New York. Dana, Lauren and Jayden drove up to join us. The first two days went well. We all cooked together and sat around playing games. After observing Dana's interaction with Jayden and Lauren, I thought they would remain together. Dana was patient with Jayden and helped and encouraged him with whatever Jayden was interested in at the time. He was more patient than the rest of us, I dare say. The boy would eat nothing but peanut butter and jelly or chicken nuggets. We all thought this was a bit over the top for a six-year-old, but we decided it wasn't our problem and if Dana could deal with it so could we. My granddaughters were not as kind to Jayden. After an argument among the children, Lauren decided to call an end to their visit after the second day and packed up to go home. I thought that strange.

By the spring of 2015, Lauren and Dana had been together a little over a year. Dana called me one morning to say he had something he wanted to run by me. A long story followed. Lauren's mother Karen was suffering from polycystic kidney disease. Her survival chances were slim if she did not receive a new kidney. Dana explained that Lauren was a blood type match, but because her sister also had the same disorder, she most likely would one day have to donate one of her kidneys to her sister. The rest of the family had been tested but none were a match. I wondered at this point where he was going with this and asked him.

"Mom, I want to donate one of my kidneys to Karen," he told me. "If I don't do this, her hopes are really slim. I want to do this for Karen and for Lauren."

"Are you kidding me?" I replied. "You don't even know what that might mean for yourself in the future. This is definitely not a good idea, Dana." I went on to explain how it might impact him physically, and how there had to be another alternative to this situation. I voiced many reasons why this was a terrible idea. We went at it for more than an hour. He kept telling me he wanted to do something for someone else for a change. After an hour I knew he was not going to change his mind.

Julina also told him it was a bad idea. Shanna tried to convince him not to do it. His dad even called and had a long talk with him, to no avail. Everyone pointed out the obvious. Perhaps one day one of our family members would have a need, we argued. Was Lauren's family then going to donate to one of us? The entire family was now on my case to jump in and say I agreed with them. I did, but I knew Dana was going to do it anyway. I wish he had not. We did not foresee what the greatest danger would be.

The transplant center, he learned, was going to need a list of medications he was on, several lab tests, and x-rays. In addition to the numerous tests he was given, he had to meet with the transplant team who included a nephrologist, a surgeon, a transplant coordinator, a social worker, a dietician, a financial counselor, and a pharmacist. This process took several months. As time went by, he seemed more and more committed to the idea. I knew he was so far into his commitment that he would not rescind his offer or change his mind.

There were many discussions with Dana and Lauren prior to the actual day of the kidney donation. Logistics had to be dealt with. My concern was who was going to care for Dana after his surgery. I felt that Lauren would have her hands full with her mother's recovery. I offered to fly up to help care for Dana, but my request fell on deaf ears. They had it all figured out, they assured me. Lauren's mother would most likely remain in the hospital for several days following the transplant, which meant that Lauren and Dana could stay at her mother's condo in Springfield while he recuperated. Lauren assured me she was most capable of handling Dana's needs. With that said, I decided not to interfere and stayed in Hilton Head.

I was waiting at home on the morning of the surgery when a weird thing happened. I turned on the "Today Show" and realized that date—December 7—was considered Giving Tuesday. *Wow,* I thought, listening to the stories of people who were giving their friends or loved ones something special. *My son is giving life. They should know about this story.* I sent an email to the producer of the show, who chose to follow up on my lead. Within a few days the following article by Amy Diluna was published on the "Today Show" website.

· · ·

Think about the nicest thing you've done for your significant other's parents. Dana Henderson can likely top it.

On Tuesday, he gave new life to his girlfriend's mother—by giving her his kidney. Karen Larsen, 61, suffers from polycystic kidney disease, a disorder that affects 1 in 500 people.

Her mother had it too, as did her mother's mother.

Karen's daughter Lauren, a records clerk for the Summit, New Jersey, Police Department, doesn't have it but her other daughter does and will likely need Lauren's kidney one day.

So when two other family member donors fell through, Henderson, a nursing student, and Lauren's boyfriend of just over a year, stepped up.

"I just think about what if it were my mom? My mom has saved my life on more than one occasion," he said. "I don't know how you don't do it."

(The story went on to say how there was a strong bond between Dana and Lauren as well as with her son Jayden.)

"We are in it for the long haul." said Henderson. "Jayden is a big part of my wanting to do this. He's so in love with his grandma and I still to this day have such a close relationship with my own grandma. He just needs her in his life I just think that' so important."

That sentiment brings Lauren to tears.

"He's an amazing person," she said. "He really is. I can't believe he's doing this, but at thesame time just knowing him for the time I've known him, I'm not surprised because he's that kind of guy."

• • •

When I read the article I was moved to tears myself. Yes, Dana had screwed up innumerable times in his life. But this kind human gesture elevated him not only in my eyes but in the eyes of his peers. A fund was set up to help with costs since he would not be able to go back to work for a while. Hundreds of people gave generously. The money would be divided between Karen and Dana.

Unfortunately, the best laid plans did not work out. Dana was released from the hospital after a successful kidney donation. He went to stay with Lauren in her mom's condo with the understanding that Karen would remain in the hospital for several days. She was released shortly after Dana, however, and wanted to go back home. This quickly created a huge problem. Naturally, Dana was in a lot of pain after the surgery. Lauren was supposed to be administering and monitoring whatever drugs he was prescribed, but this did not happen. This was my fear from the beginning. He was almost five years clean and now was having to rely on a drug for medical relief. The second problem was having Dana and Karen together in the same apartment.

Dana called me about a week after the kidney donation. This time I was happy to see his name appear on my phone because I was anxious to hear how he was doing. When I answered, I said, "Hey, Dana! So glad you called! How are you feeling?"

"Mom, this is such bullshit!!"

"What?" I replied. "What's going on?"

"It's just such bullshit!" he yelled again.

"Dana, calm down. Tell me what is happening."

"Well, I have absolutely no family here, no one to visit and . . . ."

I interrupted him. "I know, Dana, and I'm so sorry I'm not there. But Lauren told me she had it all under control."

"Mom, I know! Anyway, because I have absolutely nobody here, Joey said he would come and visit. He came over but Karen wouldn't let him in. This is such bullshit!" I could tell now he was really angry.

"Why wouldn't they let him in?" I asked.

"They're afraid of germs," he told me. "They're afraid Karen might get some sort of infection." I appreciated that concern, but this seemed a little unfair to Dana who also was recovering. Their plan was clearly not working out well.

"OK," I suggested, "why don't you and Joe just go out for a bit somewhere together? Go have lunch."

"Mom, I'm not staying here anymore. I have to get out of here!"

I felt there was something else going on but I didn't know what.

"Where would you go?"

"I'll go home, back to Dan's condo. I can't stay here anymore."

Joe offered to drive Dana back home, which he did after taking him to lunch. Joe later called to tell me Dana didn't seem normal, but he couldn't tell if it was from the medication he was prescribed after the operation or from pain.

I spoke with Dana the next day to see how he was doing. He still sounded a bit groggy but told me he was doing fine. At that point I knew he should be around family and asked if he thought he could drive. When he said he could, we decided that he would drive up to his sister's home in New York and spend a few days with her family until he felt back to normal. Julina agreed to the plan and that afternoon Dana set out for her house. The drive should have taken about an hour and fifteen minutes. Late that afternoon I called

Dana to see how he was doing. He told me he had to stop off and go shopping for something. I knew then that we had a problem because he was not acting rationally. He did not arrive at my daughter's until around 11 p.m., and she and her husband were both rightfully furious. They had been expecting him for hours and had waited up. He was not only late but he had not even called. A warm welcome was not awaiting him. I suppose because of that he slept there, but then turned around the next morning to drive back home. I wasn't quite sure what to make of all this but suspected that it was not good. He spent the next week at home recuperating.

I booked a ticket for him to fly down to Hilton Head. It was too soon for him to return to work and school was finished for the semester. It seemed he needed some recovery time. And if I was not mistaken he needed some monitoring. Lauren did not accompany him. I assumed it was because she was taking care of her mother. Dana and I spent a great week together with Shanna's family and talked about his projected path for the future. He was to return to nursing school in January. When he returned home to start his classes, I thought all was well.

At the beginning of February, I received a text from Lauren. It was lengthy, very lengthy. She told me how Dana now had a gambling problem, was losing money, and owed on his credit cards because of it. She said she had just found out. I was irate. I suspected that he was taking more of the post-surgery prescription meds than was prescribed. I knew it was imperative that he go back to his support group and asked her to please make sure he did that. I told her he didn't have to pay for that since it was part of his recovery program. I asked her to please find out where and when the sessions were and let him know. Dana had already promised me he would do this.

She replied, "I'm sorry, but I have done all I can for him. We are not speaking right now.

I have a child to protect and I don't feel it's healthy for us to be around him anymore."

When I read that text I nearly lost it. Dana had just donated a kidney to save her mother's life. He did that because he was a good person who cared for others. Now, because he had consequential issues as a result of this, he was clearly no longer useful to Lauren. I let her know that Dana had certainly not made a good choice both in his recent actions and in his choice of her. It was clear she was not ready, nor able, to emotionally support him. Of course she responded with a lengthy text defending her position, but what galled me the most was that she accused me of not caring enough for my son to fly up and be there for the kidney donation, and how she had been there for him, holding his hand while he awaited the surgery. She had told me my presence was not necessary, as she had it covered. Maybe she really did try and help him. I'll never know. By the end of February they were through. I'm glad that relationship ended when it did, as she was truly not the person Dana thought she was. Although she was out of his life, unfortunately Pandora's box had already been opened.

Julina spoke to Dana again after all the drama with Lauren and told him to just focus on school and get through the semester. He decided to change his schedule so that he could go to school during the day and work at night. I sensed he was struggling a bit. He actually called his dad, and I was told they had a nice chat. Dana filled him in on the latest events and they had some frank conversation. Dana told him that he had found a new psychiatrist who told him that he was perhaps bipolar. Dylan sent me an email explaining all of this. When I heard that theory I wasn't convinced, and I had some misgivings about why he needed another psychiatrist. Was this for pain management or psychological issues? This should have been a red flag. I should have gotten that person's name there and then and called him up. I had the power of attorney. But I didn't. I felt that Dana had been making such great progress for the past five years and didn't need an interfering Mom. By then he told me he was back to his group and I felt he had his life under control.

He then met Bethany, a pretty and intelligent girl with whom he instantly bonded. They became inseparable and in May the family all received emails from him with his new address. He was now moving in with Bethany. I called him and told him I thought it was a rather impulsive decision. He assured me it was all good and that they had discussed at length their past relationships and they were moving forward in what they both felt was an awesome new beginning. I could sense the excitement in his voice and he seemed to be the happiest he had been in years. He sent me a picture of them together and I could read the joy on his face. He also sent me pictures of their apartment and described all the decorating they were doing. He was in his element making storage cabinets and having a hand in the creation of their new environs. He was excited for me to meet her. I was delighted he finally had met someone special.

Unfortunately, when all seemed to be finally going well for me and the entire family, my brother Jim died unexpectedly at the beginning of June. I was devastated. He had recovered from a liver transplant and then experienced complications from cancer. He had been in treatment, but somehow a valve suddenly malfunctioned and he was rushed to the hospital. He didn't make it. I flew up to New Jersey for the funeral and met all of my remaining family there. I had been asked by Karen, Jim's wife, to do a eulogy. Never having done this, and not sure I could keep my composure, I wrote it out ahead of time so I could practice it.

When I arrived in New Jersey, Joe picked me up. We were still "together" at that time, if you can consider together living 800 miles apart. So, together, we drove over to Jersey City to meet Dana and his new squeeze. That was my first time meeting her and I could tell she was nervous. They showed us around their beautiful new apartment, which had a great view of the city. Their decorating efforts had paid off and it showed all the makings of a Pottery Barn photo. We set out for dinner and got drenched in the pouring rain trying to locate the restaurant. This broke the ice a bit. Then, and after a wine for both Bethany and me, we found a common topic to discuss, sewing of all things. All went smoothly from there. I liked her immediately and felt she and Dana had something special.

That evening after dinner I showed Dana the eulogy I was giving for my brother.

"Dana," I told him as I handed him the paper. "I'd like you to be familiar with this. I'm not sure I can get through this by myself. If you could please stand with me while I'm delivering it, I'll feel better. If I become undone, you can take over for me."

He read it over, looked at me, and said, "If you can do this, Mom, I'll be amazed." (My whole family knew I cried easily.) "But I know you want to try, for Uncle Jimmy and for Karen, so yes, of course I'll go and stand with you while you do it."

I was so grateful for that, to have a back-up plan, because I really didn't think I would be able to do it.

The following day the service for my brother was held. The entire family arrived, including Dana and Bethany. I thought it was admirable that she accompanied him since she didn't know my brother or even the family. It was a hell of a way for her to meet them. The service was beautiful and moving, held in a small church in their little town. Jim had loved country music and Karen had arranged for some musicians to come and play some of his favorite songs. I became emotional and wondered if I could possibly manage a eulogy. Then it was my turn. I looked over and nodded at Dana. We both stood and he followed me to the front.

I first just stood there and thought, *Dana is actually being my support system right now. This is novel and new.* I took a deep breath and plunged ahead to deliver the eulogy, relating several funny anecdotes from our childhood as well as extolling my brother's many talents and accomplishments. Perhaps because it was so personal, and I was trying to relay how I felt about Jim, to my great relief I didn't even think to get teary. I was, nevertheless, so grateful to have Dana there with me. After the service he took Bethany to meet many of the family members.

The next month Bethany and Dana decided to fly down to Hilton Head for his birthday. They didn't stay with me, but with Shanna and her family. It was great to watch their interaction with Dana's nieces. I took video after video of the girls jumping on them and splashing around the pool or doing crazy games together in the house. Considering that the girls were just three and six years old, I was impressed that both Dana and Bethany seemed to get so much enjoyment spending time with these two young ones. Quietly I was looking toward the future when they might have children of their own. Clearly they were going to be great parents.

CHAPTER 15

ANOTHER NEW ARRIVAL

AUGUST 2016 ARRIVED and I headed north again to Julina's home in New York. It was important to me to find as much time to be with family as I could. After a few days with her family, Joe and I then drove up to Vermont for a week of celebrating the christening of the sailboat my brother Craig had just spent twelve years refurbishing. He and our dad had originally spent seven years building it together in the 1970s. It was a 39-foot ferro-cement sailboat on which I had, in my youth, spent quite a bit of time sailing. Thirteen of us boarded the boat that morning and set off on a sail around Lake Champlain. I hadn't been on the boat in twenty-five years, and the moment brought back lots of memories of my times sailing with my parents when my kids were young. When the sails were hoisted I got a huge lump in my throat and my eyes welled up with tears. So many memories! We spent an entire day on the lake and were blessed by gusty winds and blue skies. I enjoyed every aspect of that week reliving memories with my brothers. It was a reminder that life did indeed offer some wonderful family moments.

Sadly, though, my positive feelings were short-lived. I should have realized by then that every time I thought life was moving along in a positive fashion, another shoe would drop. It did.

I was back home unpacking from the trip when Shanna called me. She lived just around the corner and said she wanted to come over and speak with me. This was really odd. What was going on? Normally she just texted or called me. I told her to come on over, and five minutes later she was at my house.

"Mom, I need to tell you something," she began. "I just got an email from a person named Camilla. She said she has spent years trying to find us. She tells me she is my sister."

She then showed me her phone and I read a rather poorly worded explanation of who the young woman was and the pains she had gone through to find my family. I then looked very carefully at the young woman's face. She looked almost identical to my sister-in-law at a young age. There was no doubt in my mind that this was in fact, my ex-husband's daughter. Unquestionably she was the result of the now so long ago relationship with my maid from Brazil.

I handed the phone back to Shanna and said, "That's really odd. I always thought it was a boy."

Shanna just looked at me.

"What?" I asked her. "Did you expect a different reaction? I always knew there was a child, a person. But I somehow always thought it was a boy."

Then together we looked at Camilla's picture and I told Shanna, "This girl looks almost identical to your Aunt Jane when she was younger. There is no question in my mind she is who she says she is, your half-sister."

As calm as I appeared to be, I admit I was a little shaken once Shanna left. Thirty-some years later this daughter had appeared out of nowhere in our lives. Then the emails and phone calls started. Camilla wrote that she was so excited to have finally found our family after apparently years of searching for her father. She had hopes of uniting with her father as well as her two half-sisters and brother. I came to know all this because every email was forwarded to me by my kids.

Then the soap opera began. Of course, my girls confronted their father with this new news, and at first he vehemently denied that it was his daughter. But once I had Shanna send him the photo, he knew. While all this may seem irrelevant to Dana's story, it was not. The thing is, he was astounded when he found out about Camilla. It seems he had no recollection of the kitchen conversation that one Christmas so many years ago. He had no idea this person even existed and he was reeling from the knowledge. While I had had many years to process this information, he had not. I don't know which was worse for him, the not knowing about the half-sister, or not knowing about his father.

For the next several months there were emails upon emails going back and forth between my girls, Dana, and Camilla. While she had finally found her dad, she became quite disappointed to discover he had absolutely no interest in meeting her, knowing her, or having anything to do with her. He told our three children that he feared she was going to book a ticket from Brazil and arrive on his doorstep. He finally did write to her and in his own words expressed the fact that he had no designs to be a dad to her because his "tent was full." The irony of this remark was not lost on my three kids, who for most of their adult lives had had little to no interaction with their dad. He barely knew his own grandchildren and visits were so infrequent his four granddaughters didn't have a clue as to who he was.

Dana, as well as my girls, empathized with Camilla. He was getting daily instant messages from Camilla and her husband Andre and while they were annoying to him, he did try putting himself in her shoes. He criticized his father at length for lacking empathy. Dylan refused Camilla's phone calls and Facebook messages. He had no intention of meeting her or her family, perhaps because he was angry he'd been "found out" by his own kids. He did admit Camilla was his daughter, but he insisted she was the result of an intentional pregnancy by her mother in an effort to try and break up our family-- the family that, at the time, I thought was pretty close to perfection. After a month of discussion, he finally agreed that he would meet her virtually via Skype.

I believe that was a concession to Dana's rants about how inconsiderate an individual he was. I don't believe the Skype incident ever took place, but I do know that the entire situation took a trying emotional toll on Dana. For that, I was angrier than hell.

Because the girls were already aware beforehand that a half-sibling existed, her sudden appearance was not as traumatic for them. In fact, they now refer to her jokingly as "Sissy." They told me not a week went by when then didn't get an email from their Sissy. I also felt sorry for her because her disappointment was evident. I wasn't bitter, as I had somehow known that eventually the reality of that relationship would manifest itself by the appearance of someone. I didn't feel the need to get to know her but then, bizarre as it may seem, her mom Dina, the maid, actually tried to befriend me on Facebook. No, I didn't accept. I thought it enough that she had shared my husband. Did she think we were going to be one big happy family? I couldn't seem to take care of the family I had, and now others wanted in?

Dana eventually got over his anger at his dad, or perhaps it was displaced. By Christmas they were on speaking terms. This is perhaps because I told him that if he were to return the following semester to nursing school, I was going to need some financial help from his dad. This was the first time since our divorce I had asked him for assistance. I had borne the expenses for all of Dana's nursing school obligations as well as his rehab. I phoned his dad and suggested if he was going to now be a part of Dana's life again, he needed to be realistic and realize that if Dana were truly to obtain his goals and move forward, it was going to take some assistance from him as well. I was grateful when he agreed. Dylan then reached out and sent me an email subsequent to one of his conversations with Dana. He related how Dana sounded like a totally different person than he had spoken with months earlier.

"Given Dana's age, as incredible as it may seem with all that's happened, this may be the turning point in his life," Dylan wrote to me. "I'm naturally a pessimist when it comes to human behavior and outcomes, but this time I think he may have a shot. If I thought this was a 'Hail Mary' I wouldn't be sending you a check for $4,000. Both the girls agreed, however, if 'we' were to help him it had to be with him putting 'skin in the game.' When we spoke Dana clearly understood he was on the hook and very grateful for it."

I was relieved to read this email. For the first time in many, many years I felt like I finally wasn't the only one trying to help my son get his life on track. Perhaps 2017 would be a good year.

CHAPTER 16

THE YEAR FROM HELL

THE YEAR INITIALLY started out well. Dana was now back at nursing school and still working at the hospital. He had been working there almost five years as a technician and had made numerous friends. He was still living with Bethany in Jersey City. I spoke with him every week or so to check in. Then toward the middle of February he told me he had gone to a different doctor who told him he was bipolar and prescribed a treatment drug. He was not to be taking any type of potentially addictive drugs, and he assured me it was not. He eventually called his dad in April and told him the same thing. He also told Dylan he was on his way to meet a new psychiatrist. Just to be clear, I wasn't happy to hear that Dana was again meeting with multiple doctors. Hoping that this one had some positive thoughts to share with Dana, though, I let it go. Dana already knew the ramifications of taking too much of a prescribed drug. He had a lot at stake.

I knew by this point that Dana was having difficulties in a couple of his classes and was under a lot of pressure. He knew he couldn't fail. He would be letting a lot of people down, including himself. He was all too aware that for the first time his dad had actually helped with the tuition and he didn't want to disappoint him. The relationship between him and Bethany evidently got very strained. In addition to the pressure of his studies, he always had money concerns. I sent numerous checks to cover expenses when I learned that Bethany was being more than generous with her contributions. The financial stress was growing and causing a real strain on their relationship. Dana was trying to do his part but keeping the hours he needed to at the hospital, going to class, and keeping on top of his studies was wearing on him. By March he was considering leaving his job at the hospital. He called me and told me he thought that he could concentrate more on his studies if he left his job there and returned to his former job at the restaurant. He also tried to convince me that he could make more money at the restaurant. I detected a flaw in this seemingly well laid plan. Why would he want to backtrack on his career path at this point?

On May 11 he resigned his position at the hospital. On a Facebook post on that day he told his friends and coworkers that he wanted to "clear his head and finish what I started years ago, which is nursing school." I listened to all the reasons and rationalizations but wasn't convinced that this was the right decision. Bethany wasn't pleased with the plan either. I am sure she felt more and more financial pressure on her. I didn't ask, but the results were apparent. Shortly afterwards Dana was in search of a new place to live.

Since he now didn't have a roommate, his options were extremely limited. He searched and searched for an affordable apartment within commuting distance to his work and school. We spoke for what seemed hours about his search. The best place he could find was an apartment in Newark. This city has affectionately been named the armpit of the east and not without reason. This was the last place I wanted to see him live. After describing the place he had found, he said it needed paint. *Oh great!* I thought, *Here we go again with the painting!* I was more concerned about the fact that he was in Newark, with no garage for his car, which by the way, was in my name as well. He signed a short-term lease, moved in and managed to fix the place up to his liking then sent me photos. I suggested he concentrate a little more on his schoolwork than his environs. But at least he was settled.

"Just study," I told him over and over. "Just concentrate on finishing your program." He was so close to the end and I didn't want to see anything jeopardize his chances of finishing nursing school.

In June he called me frantically. His "now not-girlfriend-anymore" Bethany had been taken to the hospital. Very concerned, he went to see her and, as a result of this, he was late showing up for his job at the restaurant. They fired him. It seemed now he was out of a job and had no way to pay his bills or his rent. I was on the hook again.

A few weeks later, when it seemed things could not get any worse, I received another phone call from him. Again, the news was not good. He told me his car had been stolen. He told me it had been parked in front of his apartment and the next day he went out and it was gone. I asked him if he had reported it to the police and he told me he had. He had walked to the police station and filed a report that day. He was also upset because now he had no way to try and get another job. He was to have had an interview that afternoon with another restaurant. He eventually got to the restaurant by Uber but did not get the job. Things were clearly not on a good path right now. About four or five days passed, and finally the police called him and told him they had found his car. It was found abandoned in some parking lot riddled with bullet holes. I heard that in its heyday Newark truly was a lovely city. Not so much now.

The bad luck all took place at the end of June. His semester had ended for the spring. The original plan was to have all the family, including Dana—but now not Bethany—meet up at Julina's for the Fourth of July. I figured it would be a good break for Dana, having just gone through the month from hell. Maybe we could all shed some perspective on his life, which seemed to be going awry. I flew up to Newark and Joe picked me up.

While I was in the car heading out of the airport, Dana called to tell me he had decided to go to the lot where the police had told him his car had been abandoned. He wanted to see if his golf clubs were still in the car. As he walked through the parking lot he had me on speaker phone and described how the lot was located in a terrible area next to some abandoned warehouses. He then proceeded to take pictures of the car and send them to me. The two-year-old car appeared to be about fifteen. It was indeed riddled with bullet holes and had clearly been in a collision. If I had to guess, someone had stolen it and was involved in some sort of drug run—conjecture on my part, but totally realistic considering where he was. When I asked him who was around there, he told me he saw no one on the lot but could see a group of guys gathered in the adjacent lot. Now my angst rose and I told him to get the hell out of there. He did, but only after he successfully retrieved his golf clubs, which were amazingly still in the trunk of the car. Whoever had stolen the car was either high or stupid or both. The clubs were worth quite a bit of money. They were also the only thing of any value that Dana owned at the time. Truly depressing.

At my request, Dana had called the insurance company earlier that week to report his car stolen. They then told him he did not have comprehensive insurance. When he called to tell me this news, I was with clients. I took the call outside the home I was showing them and hit the ceiling. This was unbelievable. How did he not have proper insurance? Somehow, after many phone calls, that got resolved and his coverage was put in place. The totally destroyed car had about $16,000 of payments yet due. Without coverage, I would have been responsible. He called them again after the car was located and they said they would send an adjuster out to assess the damages. They didn't say when. Dana decided at that point he was not going to join us for the Fourth of July celebration in New York. He was going to try and resolve the whole car issue.

After that discussion, I resolved that Dana would come down and spend the summer with me. He had no job, no girlfriend, his apartment was in the middle of a hellhole, and his car was completely destroyed. I figured he could use a change. His life was a far cry from where we had hoped it would be. I called him back and told him my plan. He agreed and said he would speak to his landlord and then, after he had resolved the car issue, would head down to Hilton Head. That would take some time.

The insurance adjuster finally showed up on the lot three days later. He called me and said he felt the car could be fixed and where did I wanted it towed? I explained that I was in South Carolina but had a shop in Summit I liked where it could be towed and repaired. I thought this was an exercise in futility. After having seen the pictures Dana had taken, I wasn't sure the car could ever be properly fixed, but arguing with an insurance adjuster is totally useless.

After another day, the shop called me and said the adjuster was quite mistaken. His numbers were far from the realistic amount it would take to repair the car properly. They declared it a total loss. No surprise there. Now Dana had nothing to drive and no way to get down to South Carolina. We decided he would rent a car, until the insurance company could resolve the issue. I told Dana to get a car and head down as soon as he could. I could not wait for him to leave the Garden State. If I had my way, he would not be returning there anytime soon.

He was to have left on a Friday. He couldn't, he told me. He had a lot of packing to do. On Saturday he said he had spoken to his landlord and apparently his landlord wasn't happy with the color Dana had painted the apartment, so he was going to have to repaint it before he left. This was not good for so many reasons. He didn't have money for paint and by his voice I could tell he was a bit stressed out about all that had happened. I urged him to get on with it and just get down to Hilton Head. He said he would. Apparently, the painting took on a life of its own. I later discovered that he had made a bit of a mess of it, evidenced by the amount of paint on every article of clothing he owned. By Monday he had made some progress and thought he would be leaving on Tuesday.

Tuesday morning arrived and he said he was finally packed and ready to go. It is a twelve-hour drive from New Jersey to Hilton Head and I expected him to arrive by dinner time. When the hour came and went and I hadn't heard from him, I called his cell phone around 8 p.m. He told me he had taken a detour over to Myrtle Beach on the way to see some friends. This, too, was not good. Remembering all that had occurred in Myrtle Beach, I became annoyed and anxious. I told him I saw no reason for this detour, and he needed to get back on the road and get to my house. I called Shanna and told her where he was. We had both been monitoring his progress, or lack of it. Given that it is about a four-hour drive from Myrtle Beach to Hilton Head, Shanna thought it best for Dana to drive to her house instead as he would get in late and she didn't want me staying up waiting for him. They were younger and used to late hours. I was getting older by the minute, so I agreed and went to bed.

The next morning I got up and dressed for my weekly golf game without checking in with Shanna. It was early and assumed they had been up late waiting for Dana. As I was getting out of my car, though, I saw an incoming call from Shanna on my cell phone. Glad to hear some news, I answered and asked her what time Dana had arrived.

"Mom, that's what I'm calling to tell you. He never arrived. I haven't heard from him since last night and I have no idea where he is. He's not answering his cell phone. I've tried him all morning, too. Now I'm worried."

At this, my anxiety level went through the roof. Where the hell was he? Now I was worried and so was Shanna. She suggested I contact the state police. I immediately got back in my car and told her I would meet her at a nearby gas station where we could figure out what to do next. We didn't want this conversation taking place in front of her children. When I arrived there I parked and tried to collect myself. I had no idea where my son was or where to start looking. I was totally stressed out and needed to calm down. As I sat there, I realized that before I could even call the police, I had to know what kind of car he was driving. As he had rented a car, I didn't have a clue what he had. Where could I start?

First I called the insurance company, thinking maybe he had contacted them to rent the car. After speaking with about six different people I was finally able to determine the make and model of the car. It was a black Chevy sedan. Great, like there weren't a million black cars out there. It took me five more phone calls to finally determine what the license plate was on the car. Finally, I was able to contact the police. They wanted to know his last known location. I had no idea. I told them I would call them back.

In the meantime, Shanna had been phoning Dana's friends to find out if he had been in contact with any of them. She finally spoke with his friend Dave, who said Dana had called him at 1 a.m. asking for gas money. Dave said he would wire some money and Dana could pick it up at a Walmart. He thought Dana was somewhere in South Carolina, perhaps Walterboro. But that was far north and we didn't know if he had traveled farther south. I relayed this information to the police and told them Dana had driven through Myrtle Beach and most likely was somewhere on or near Interstate 95. We had no idea where to begin.

Both Shanna and I were beside ourselves. We knew we had to find him. We kept trying his cell phone, but he wasn't answering.

We decided to try the nearest Walmart located off the island. Maybe he had gotten there and fallen asleep in his car. We drove out there and cruised through the entire parking lot for about a half-hour with no luck. We then headed out to I-95. Guessing maybe he had missed the exit for the island, we drove south to where we knew another Walmart was located, just north of Savannah. Maybe he really was in Georgia. All kinds of thoughts were going through our minds. We couldn't figure out why we hadn't heard from him. Maybe he had been in an accident and no one had seen it. We tried not to believe the worst. I just drove, clutching the wheel and trying to focus on the road. We finally reached the Walmart near Savannah and cruised through that parking lot to no avail.

Just as we were leaving, we received a text from Dana's ex-girlfriend Bethany. We had called her hours before and left a message at her work. Had she spoken with Dana? She was finally texting to suggest I call his phone company to request a GPS of his cell phone. She told me his phone was definitely on, but she didn't have his Apple ID. She said if she heard from him she would let me know.

By the time Bethany called us again it was after noon. We had been driving around for nearly four hours. She told us he was sleeping in the car. At least we now knew he was alive, but we still didn't know where he was. About thirty minutes later we heard from him. He sounded disoriented and told us he wasn't sure where he was. Shanna then led him through the process of setting his location on her cell phone. He told us his phone was nearly dead, but we had a location. He was a good two hours north of us on I-95 on the side of the road. He had no gas. We had had no response from the police. We decided to go find him ourselves.

It was the middle of July and was almost 100 degrees that day. We assumed that if Dana had no gas, he quite possibly had no water or food either. When we finally neared the area where the locator indicated he would be, we realized he was on the southbound lane. This meant we had to travel another ten miles north before we could turn around. This was agonizing, passing the location on the other side where we knew he was and not being able to reach him yet. We made a quick stop for water and bought a gas can and filled it with gas.

"That's odd," the woman at the Quick Stop told us. "There was a young man in here last night who needed gas but didn't have enough money to buy the can."

Oh my Lord, I thought, *that was Dana*. The fact that he had been there meant he had walked from his car back up to the gas station. Even worse, he would have had to cross I-95 on foot, at night. The thought was horrifying.

Gas and water in hand, we sped back down I-95. We finally spotted the car pulled off to the side. Next to the car we saw Dana, lying on a blanket on the side of the road. He got up and looked awful. As I walked toward him I noticed he had shaved off all his hair.

He was barely recognizable with his pants hanging on him, wearing no shirt or shoes. His eyes were bleary. He looked like a homeless person. I just stared at him. This young man—my son, whom I was about to embrace—was a stranger to me.

"Mom, I know I look weird," he said. "I shaved off all my hair because it became too hot up there. It's easier to take care of this way."

"Well, you look like hell," I replied. "What is going on?"

He already knew we had been looking for him for hours. "I ran out of gas and my phone had practically no service. I tried to charge it but now I think the battery on the car is dead."

At that moment a state trooper pulled up behind us. *Great timing!* I thought. *Where had he been hours ago?* Apparently, someone had called in seeing a body stretched out along the side of the highway, so he had come to investigate. We explained that Dana had run out of gas and now found his battery was dead. At least the trooper was helpful. Had he arrived before us, I don't know what the outcome would have been. He told us where we could buy a battery charger twenty miles down the highway, so we left the car, took Dana, and headed out to find one. We bought the charger and returned to the car only to find that the charger was defective. Nothing was easy, it seemed. We had to return to the store for another. I didn't want to chance jumper cables because there was no way to maneuver my car to the front of his on the side of the interstate without risking getting hit head-on by someone. Once we arrived back at his abandoned car, it took us nearly another hour to charge the battery in the scorching heat while cars and large trucks whizzed past us at 80-90 miles per hour. Way too close for comfort. We were exhausted and hungry. Once the car was fired up, I had Shanna drive Dana's car and follow me back. He didn't seem in any condition to drive. Dana rode with me and I tried to make sense of the past twenty-four hours by grilling him with questions. He fell asleep.

It was after 5:30 by the time we got back to Hilton Head. Shanna had missed a day at work and her husband Mike had had to come home to mind their girls. We were all pretty pissed. Relieved, but pissed. Dana awoke once we crossed the bridge to the island, but I could tell he was drained. We returned to the gas station where Shanna had left her car early that morning. Dana was now awake and coherent, so I figured he could at least drive his car the three miles from there to my house. I told Shanna I would check in with her later.

When I reminded Dana that he needed to show his driver's license in order to get a gate pass into my gated community, he looked for it. He couldn't find it in his pocket, which is where he told me he had it after getting stopped by the police sometime the evening before. This I hadn't known. Would this nightmare never end? I never knew why they stopped him or why they let him drive away. He's a good storyteller. Not finding the license, he then proceeded to drag everything out of his trunk looking for it. We now had a homeless-looking person with crap strewn all over the parking lot of the gas station. My day was not getting any better. Eventually he found it in another pocket. I remember thinking that it had taken him three days to "pack?" That thought then stopped me in my tracks. It was then that I realized that these were his belongings. These were *all* of his belongings. Everything else he owned had been left in New Jersey, or had it? Where were his books, mementos, trophies? What had happened to all the wonderful items for his apartment he had made or accumulated? His life was there on the ground in front of us.

Sighing, I asked Dana if he remembered how to get to my house. He did. I got home ten minutes later, but fifteen minutes went by and he still wasn't there. I called his cell phone, which now had a charge. He was lost in the neighborhood and I had to direct him in. I suspected this was going to be a very long summer.

When he finally got to my house he unloaded a few things, telling me he would unpack tomorrow. I gave him some dinner and he went to bed, visibly exhausted. At least now he was safe. He slept until noon the next day and, when he finally did get up, we had a discussion about what he might do for the summer. He thought he would apply for a job at one of the restaurants. Seeing as how there are more than 200 on the island, all busy during the summer, this seemed like a good idea.

The following day he seemed much better. After a good sleep, a shower, and some good food his appearance wasn't nearly as disturbing. He still looked unfamiliar with a shaven head though. After breakfast he set off for an interview and returned home saying that it had gone well and that they would get back to him. OK, there was progress. When I asked about what the hell had happened on the way down, he told me he had taken too much of his medication (which was prescribed by his doctor for his ADHD condition) to stay awake. He promised me and swore up and down he was not abusing drugs again. I wanted to believe him. Shanna and Mike didn't and warned me. I said I was going to keep a close watch and make sure he wasn't. Mike decided to come over while Dana was gone and go through his things and his car. All he found was his prescriptions, both prescribed by a psychiatrist.

The following day he went to see about a position at yet another restaurant. *This was good,* I thought. *He's really trying.* Later on we had a long sit-down. I told him he was going to have to be productive that summer and earn some money if he wanted to return to nursing school. I also told him I expected him to help with chores around the house, including mowing the grass, doing his laundry, and keeping his room clean which was still in a state of utter turmoil, backpacks thrown around and clothes all over the place. He agreed to all of this, of course. Mom was giving him free rent and food.

Fast forward to that evening. Dana decided after dinner that he wanted to go and hit some range balls. I thought, *Why not? At lease he'll be outside getting some exercise.* Hours went by and I knew the range had closed. Now where was he? It was like having a runaway dog. I called Shanna to see if he was over there. No, she hadn't seen him. About another hour went by and finally he arrived home around 10 p.m. He had decided to retrieve golf balls from some of the lagoons around the course. While this may seem like a good idea in theory, it's actually quite dangerous. Our lagoons are filled with alligators anxious to protect their babies, and they aren't partial to allowing people to go poking around their turf. I also wasn't keen on the fact that he had been fishing around in the lagoons at my club where he wasn't a member, and I could foresee all kinds of potential ramifications for him and me if he had been caught. I told him so. Day two of the summer wasn't going too well. I decided to go to bed and told him to do the same. He didn't.

The next morning I went out to my garage and discovered that chaos had struck there. My kayaks were now hanging from hooks on the wall, well above my reach so there was no way I could get them down. Lots of things had been moved around. There were nails, nuts, bolts, and tools strewn everywhere. It looked like Dana had decided on another project. Oh, crap! That was too reminiscent of the past. I marched back into the house to confront him, but he was sound asleep. I decided to wait until later. A great start to day three.

When I returned home later that day, we had yet another talk. He told me he was trying to help by organizing the garage and thought it would give me more space if he hung some things up.

"What about the cleanup part don't you get?" I asked him.

He told me that by the time he finished it was about 3 a.m. and he was really tired so decided to go to bed. He promised to clean it up that evening. Maybe he was really trying to help and I was overreacting. But I also was becoming suspicious and apprehensive. What if he was lying? What if he was now using again?

I had been invited to a birthday celebration dinner that evening and was trying to decide whether I should go. It finally occurred to me that I couldn't sit around all summer to babysit my now thirty-four-year-old son. He would be OK for an evening on his own. I made him a quick dinner before I left and told him to please clean up his room and the garage. I went to the dinner but couldn't shake the feeling that something was off. I was not relaxed and barely spoke a word with my friends, who could detect something was wrong. As soon as we finished the meal I excused myself and left. I headed home to check on Dana. He wasn't at home. The garage was still a mess and so was his room.

Well, maybe he went to the range again. Or maybe he was getting more golf balls. That I doubted. He already had enough to supply the PGA tour. He was on the loose again to God knows where. I called Shanna. Nope, he wasn't there. This was getting old. It was several hours before he got home. He said he had been trying to get a job. At night? I suspected not, but I was running out of energy to ask questions. Trusting him was proving to be difficult.

Saturday was day four. Hopefully this would prove to be a better day. We all had dinner at Shanna's and Mike's. Shanna was pretty pissed at Dana because he still had made no acknowledgement or thanks for the ordeal that he had put us all through that Wednesday. The event remained the elephant in the room that everyone ignored. They discussed his possible job opportunities for the summer and which venues might be the best fit for him. I left for home before Dana and left them to it. Four days of Dana had exhausted me.

The next day Shanna called me, and this time she was really angry. She, Mike, and the girls had gone out for a bit. When they returned home they found Dana in their house.

"OK," I said, "so did he know you were not home?"

"Yes, he knew. But we came home early. Mom, he said he was here to look for his shoes which he forgot last night. But we found him in the bathroom. There is no way he was looking for his shoes."

"OK, what are you telling me, Shanna?'

"I'm telling you, Mom, that he was looking for drugs!"

CHAPTER 17

HERE WE GO AGAIN

AFTER CONFRONTING DANA with his "walkabout" in Shanna's house in what she thought was the pursuit of drugs, I decided to check out his room yet again. I found a vial of a prescribed drug I had obtained from my doctor the year before after an operation I had undergone. Now I was seething mad. When I asked him about it, he told me he needed something for a headache. Not likely, I thought. After this discovery he knew he didn't have a leg to stand on. I knew then we had a decision to make. It had been five years. We were now back to square one. He was using again.

He had promised never again. How totally depressing was this? This time I knew without a doubt that whatever support system he had been depending on had failed. This time I wasn't there. While all parents of addicts know they can't be there all the time, we all, I am sure, wish we could be. I wasn't blaming myself this time. I thought he had all the tools necessary to deal with his problem. Apparently not. His addiction had won. The following day I spent agonizing over the decision. Where could he go? Where was the best place to help him? He was now living with me in South Carolina and I didn't have a clue about the available facilities in my area. And what was the cost? Did

Dana have any kind of insurance to help cover a stay in rehab? As it turned out, he did have insurance, but unfortunately he wasn't covered in South Carolina. I knew his dad wasn't going to pay to help. He had already made it clear when he helped with Dana's tuition that it was Dana's last chance. I knew I was on my own for what was bound to be another expensive proposition. Again, I couldn't even consider turning my back and not helping him.

I told him, "Dana, this absolutely has to be the last time. You can do this. You *have* to do this. This is your life we're talking about. I can help you but you really have to *want* this."

After researching online for an eternity, I found possibilities. The first was a facility that took patients for no less than six months. It was a rehab program which then transitioned into a work program. This sounded good on paper, but I was concerned about sending him away for six months. Dana and I talked at length about this, neither one of us wanting to see him go for that amount of time. Ultimately, he told me that he would agree to whatever I thought best. After further research I found out that some of the staff at this facility were not the most stable themselves, so that choice was off the table.

An easy decision would have been option two. There was a facility on the island only two miles from my house. Perfect! It turned out the cost was in excess of $10,000 for one month, which was not perfect. I was working only part-time and did not have an abundance of money. I had been hoping to have a pool built on my property. Apparently that plan was to be shelved. It was more important that Dana got the help he needed. Back to do more research.

That day seemed like Groundhog's Day to me. Five years earlier I had been through this same unnerving experience and didn't feel any more confident the second time around making this tough decision. Further research finally revealed a facility that had recently opened its doors upstate. I tried to search for online reviews, but there were none. I called the facility and spoke to some of the staff there and asked why no reviews were to be found. That's when they told me they were brand new. This was a crapshoot, but it was in-state and a lot more affordable. I was beginning to think it was easier to find a college for your kid than a rehab facility, but after we spoke I felt more comfortable and the decision was made. I told him to go pack, again. We were leaving the next morning.

When we arrived after a two-hour drive upstate, we were quite impressed. The facility was located in the middle of nowhere (*good!*) and had an air of tranquility. We were told it had formerly been used as a hunting retreat for some famous person. The facility sat on beautifully maintained grounds with a pond and surrounded by woods. All the buildings were new or newly renovated. We took in the surroundings and went in search of the administration building. Next step: register and get evaluated. Check, check. Then there was an explanation of the program itself and common causes for relapses, followed by writing the necessary checks and the promise of future payments. Would this never end? We finally said our goodbyes, with my parting words something to the effect of, "This is your last chance. Don't screw it up." I am sure every parent who has ever experienced this nightmarish situation said exactly the same. My mental health and my bank account could take no more.

I dropped him off on a Wednesday. That was day seven of his "not to be" summer with me. I knew I wouldn't see him until the end of August at best. I drove home totally depressed, but I would have to think about something else. I couldn't wait to get home. I needed to unwind and de-stress. Wednesdays were my country line dancing nights, a pastime I found to be great exercise as well as therapeutic, helping me cope with Dana's addiction in so many ways. I needed to dance mindlessly and not dwell on the events of the week. I was looking forward to seeing my friends that evening and, when I arrived, one look at me told them something was up. I confided in one of them who also had a son with an addiction. We parents seem to find each other. That's a good thing. We need all the support we can get. Having another person understand what you are going through when you have put one of your offspring in rehab for a second time is somehow reassuring. You don't feel so alone. She and I would do a lot of talking in the months to come.

So there I was again, living my worst nightmare. While every story is different, the result is the same. The parents suffer tremendously. The mental anguish never subsides, always wondering if you could have done yet something else to prevent this from happening yet again. Dana had been clean for five years. I was determined to find out the cause of the reoccurrence.

After a week, I was allowed to visit Dana. The two-hour drive became three as I encountered accident after accident. But the drive time gave me time to formulate some questions for him. I wanted some alone-time with him to hash out the recent events of his life. On my way up he called me. Could I please bring milk? Odd, I thought, milk? Why? He wanted at least two gallons. I stopped to get it at the Walmart whose parking lot I had recently cruised through frantically looking for his car. This just evoked bad memories.

When I arrived at the rehab center, I was greeted with cheers by him and his newly found friends. It seemed because the facility was new, there was no kitchen yet on the premises. All the food was ordered off "campus" and brought in. The patients loved their cereal but never had enough milk. They also were craving fresh fruit. Upon discovering this and hearing complaints from all his friends, I had some words with the management. Nutrition was a key to their health and wellbeing and at the price I and other families were paying, we expected more. If I could assist in helping in the smallest way to foster that, I gladly would. Fortunately that was to be the only complaint I had with the facility during the time of Dana's stay. They really did have a terrific program.

After meeting his friends, taking a tour of his room, and chatting with some of the staff we went for a walk around the premises. He told me how sorry he was that he had ended up there and all he had put me through. He then went on to say how much better off he thought he was than several of his new friends there. Some were addicted to heroin, an older one had been an alcoholic for twenty years, and another had tried to take her own life. No names were mentioned. They were just people he had met.

I stopped and looked at him and said: "Dana, the fact that you are here means you have your own huge problem. Do not diminish that. We need to talk about why you relapsed. If we don't, the odds of it happening again are extremely likely. I know there were triggers."

We had learned that triggers are social, environmental, or emotional situations that remind people in recovery of their past drug addiction. These cues bring about urges that can lead to a relapse. While triggers do not force a person to use drugs, they increase the likelihood of drug use. I had also learned that long-term drug use creates an association in the brain between daily routines and drug experiences. A recovering addict can suffer from uncontrollable drug cravings when exposed to certain cues. The cravings then act as a reflex to certain internal or external triggers. This response can affect addicts who had abstained from drugs for a long time. It was critical that we discussed his triggers. I knew he would be doing that in his group sessions, but I needed to know to understand and be able to help him.

"Mom," he sighed, "there were so many things. First was the pressure of school. I was trying really hard and knew that both you and dad wanted me to do well. I stopped gambling as soon as I moved in with Bethany. I was trying so hard to make money to help her. I was putting a lot of pressure on myself. Then Bethany put additional pressure on me and said if I did not successfully pass the semester she was through with me and I would have to move out. She felt like she had given it enough time. So when I failed the semester course, she said that was it. That's why I had to find another place."

OK, this I had not known. I only knew that Dana had loved this girl and was pretty devastated when they split up. But he continued when I asked him if there was anything else.

"Oh, yeah. I have spent months trying to come to grips with what dad did. I never knew anything about that. You told me the girls knew and yet you never told me. I find out when I am thirty-four years old I have a half-sister which I never knew anything about! Why wasn't I told?"

Evidently this had been on his mind more than I had realized.

"Dana, you were told. You just don't remember. We were all at my house for Christmas six or seven years ago. We were all talking about it. Apparently, you didn't pay attention." *Or,* I thought to myself, *you were on drugs.*

"Well it really unnerved me," he went on. "I felt like I had been left out of a really important family occurrence. I felt excluded. I was feeling depressed as hell and that didn't help at all." He went on to describe his many emails with his dad after finding out and expressed his disappointment over how his dad had handled the situation. Apparently, the emails did not foster a better relationship between father and son.

Then he went on. "I was living in Newark in this horrible place, by myself, no family, no friends, and no one to talk to."

I asked about his support group. He had stopped going to that, which was a major problem. One can never, never stop attending meetings. An addict never recovers. This, coupled with the fact he had no support group whatsoever, made me realize then that I did not want him to return to that environment under any circumstances. But then I asked about the drugs. He finally admitted that after he had donated the kidney to his ex-girlfriend's mother, he had started using again. Not a lot, just enough to get him through his classes and his shifts. I was not surprised at this news, but was totally annoyed. This is what we had all feared. Having a major operation with no drugs is virtually impossible. Just taking some to alleviate the pain set off the cravings for more. He had done a truly altruistic thing and it had contributed to his relapse.

I asked him about quitting his job at the hospital and he admitted that if he hadn't quit they would most likely have fired him. He thought they suspected that he had been using something. Had he been fired, he never would have been able to get a job in nursing. He admitted to the stupidity of it all.

"Well, Dana," I said, "if you are really committed to being a nurse, you are going to have to make some drastic changes. As a nurse, having access to drugs could continue to be a problem. If you really want to become a nurse, you are going to have to find a way to cope with your anxieties and problems. When you get out of here you know what you have to do. Meetings are mandatory and you're going to need to find a sponsor who can help you. I'll be there for you, but it won't be enough."

I was thinking that the best thing for him to do when he was released was to move back in with me. I felt it best for him to stay in South Carolina where at least he had me and his sister's family nearby. There he could have a support group and family. I was determined not to have him return to New Jersey where, in my mind, all bad things had occurred. I mentioned this to him and he didn't think it was a bad idea. However, there was the problem of school. His program was in New Jersey. We weren't sure if his credits would transfer to a South Carolina nursing program. This was another obstacle to cross.

On my drive back home I reflected on our conversation. I realized, after putting the pieces together, I should have seen it coming. It appeared that a relapse was inevitable. He had had every social, emotional, and environmental element in his life turned sideways. He had had no support. As a recovering addict he was in every way doomed from the start. He had sought the help of psychiatrists in New Jersey, but they were only willing to supply yet more drugs that he had been substituting to overcome his triggers. This strengthened my distrust of psychiatrists, although Dana would insist they helped. Look where he was, again. Yet I was not naïve enough to think this was not Dana's fault. He had made bad choices and never should have left his group.

When I returned home I realized I was now going to have to deal with the issue of his rental car, which sat in my driveway. Clearly, he would have no use for this as he was going nowhere soon. I called the company. I could return it nearby, on the island, but first it had to be cleaned out.

Upon inspection I found the flooring in the trunk had been removed. *Drugs in there?* I found random articles of clothing, shoes, the odd slipper, tool parts, food remnants, painting materials, golf balls, and the lot. Truly a homeless shelter, if you ask me. It took hours to clean out and put to rights. Then I discovered a huge scratch on the side and one near the gas cap. Totally exasperated, I set off to the store to try and buy some car paint so at least I could make it look presentable. It didn't turn out well, but I tried. When I returned the car to Enterprise, the young man was very nice. He could tell I was rather anxious and distraught. One look at my now-haggard face indicated that recent events had taken a toll on me. He pointed out the scratch and said it looked like someone tried to fix it. I tried to look shocked. He pointed to the one near the gas cap.

"That's Jersey for you," I tried to explain. (The car had Jersey plates.) "They don't let you pump your own gas there. They're in such a hurry! It looks like someone just whipped it out of there and scratched it."

He just looked at me and said it was fine. I could just leave. Thank you, whoever you were. You made a very bad week just a wee bit better.

Having dealt with the car, it was now time to tackle his room. Well, it was a room in my house but Dana had been using it for nearly a week and it needed some tending to. No, it was a complete disaster. When I started sorting out his strewn clothing, I noticed nearly every article was covered with orange paint. I found out later this was a result of his "repainting" experience before exiting his apartment in Newark. I can only imagine what that looked like. How he managed to get it on pillows and a bed comforter is beyond me. Did I mention the dried-out paint brushes were in the car? Lovely. I loved my son, but so help me God he was trying my patience at this point.

His phone had been left at my house as no cell phones were allowed in rehab. He had asked me to please not look through it. I thought for a moment about that, but then did anyway. I felt I had a right to know what had led up to this recent hellish fiasco that I was now not only cleaning up, but paying for as well. So scroll and search I did, especially the texts. I was trying to figure out what had gone on during that last week. The only thing of importance I discovered was that he had, perhaps, a new girl in his life. That is when I first learned about Colleen.

CHAPTER 18

MY HALFWAY HOUSE

AT THE END of August it was finally time for him to come home. I drove to his rehab facility to pick him up in the used automobile I had bought for him. He had to have something to drive and there was no public transportation on the island. The car was put in my name. There were to be no more car leases and no more rent for which I was on the hook. And hopefully no more rehab costs (for which I was still on the hook).

Once home, we had a long conversation about the rules. We always seemed to have long conversations. But there had to be rules. I was going to be his Halfway House for the duration of the year. We discussed the money situation, of which he had none, I might add. But we decided whatever he did earn was to go to me for expenses and I would give him an allowance for his gas and incidentals. Then there was the question of what he was going to do for the rest of the year. Heal and recover. That was the first priority.

A friend of mine recommended a group called YANA which was very close by. This acronym stands for You Are Not Alone. Dana attended meetings daily, sometimes twice a day. They were welcoming and he made many friends. He had a great support group.

I cannot say enough about this wonderful organization, which offers so much help and support to recovering addicts. There were and still are, over thirty meetings held per week. Despite the number of tourists, Hilton Head is a small island. If that number is not an indicator of the ever-growing problem of addiction then I don't know what is.

I had been hoping during this recovery time that Dana might decide to catch up on his studies and made this suggestion. He had failed his last course the past semester when he was living in Newark and there was no way he would be returning to school that fall. My suggestion fell on deaf ears and then I finally realized that studying was more than he could process. He needed to first get himself in the right mindset. He landed a job working part time for one of the golf groups, which gave him some structure as well as spending money. It also allowed him time to attend the meetings at YANA. This was his major priority for the first three months. Having a car enabled him to also do some Ubering to earn some additional money.

In addition to the support offered to him by his family and YANA, I give a large portion of the credit to his new friend Colleen. Once he returned to my home they spoke every day. I had not met her and only knew that they had seen each other just a few times before Dana departed for his nightmarish trip to Hilton Head. Their "relationship" was confined to the phone at this point. They spoke every day, much to her credit. I didn't think it was going anywhere. I wanted him to stay in South Carolina.

The future loomed hazy in his mind. Returning to nursing school was a question we needed to address. A major concern expressed by the entire family was whether he should even continue in this course of study. The access he would always have to drugs was indisputable. Would he have learned enough or have the ability to resist the urge when he had such ready access? After much debate and many discussions, he announced that he did want to finish the program and get his nursing degree.

Eventually we decided to investigate having him transfer his credits to the nearby University of South Carolina's Beaufort campus. The last thing I wanted was for him to return to New Jersey to finish his program. After checking it out he found out he would lose too many credits. Now what? We had time to think about it. He could not return to school until the following January anyway.

Having Dana stay with me that summer was a different experience than when he was younger. While I went about my life, work, and the various sports I played, I always had half an eye on him. I wanted to trust him, but life had taught me not to be caught unaware of what might happen. I was relieved he was with me, but probably anxious most of the time. We made healthy meals together and played some golf when we were able. He gained some weight and improved both physically and mentally. Having family around him seemed to be helping a lot. Julina and her family came to visit in July and I was encouraged to see him engage with all his nieces as well as with his brothers-in-law. We were trying to create normal.

It was interesting and eye-opening to see how some of my friends handled the situation of my son staying with me. I referred to my home as the "halfway house" which, in essence, it was. As we occasionally went to my club and played golf with some of my friends, he had the opportunity to get to know them. Several asked constantly how he was doing and seemed genuinely interested in his progress. There were one or two though who, to my disappointment, treated him as if he had the plague. On one occasion we played a round of golf with a person who spoke not a word to my son the entire afternoon. Dana commented on this afterwards, to which I replied, "She doesn't have children. She just doesn't know what to say." I wasn't defending her, just making a lame excuse, I guess. But it is hurtful to a mom to think that a "friend" doesn't find it worth her time to even engage your son in a conversation because he has a "problem." Unfortunately in society, for those families who have either a special-needs child or an addict, this is a common occurrence. When one enters a room, some people avert their eyes. Fortunately this is not always true. For the most part my friends were encouraging and supportive during that entire time. They became my support group. Dana had his. I needed mine as well.

Fall arrived and the end of the year was fast approaching. As it seemed he was mentally ready to take on challenges again, we discussed the alternatives for the next semester. He was keen on finishing his nursing degree. After much debate, and with much reluctance, I finally agreed to let him return to New Jersey to finish his program. The condition was, however, that he had to get a room on campus. No roommates, no cheap, seedy apartment, and close to his classes. This seemed like the best alternative. It was not only affordable, but it seemed practical as well. After checking with the school we learned that those arrangements could be made.

Dana and I were planning on driving north for the holidays as I wanted the family to be together. Julina and Doug were having Christmas at their home in New York. My thought was to drive up in my car and then return home as his semester didn't start until the second week of January. He argued he didn't want to turn around after the holidays and drive up by himself. After reflecting on his last solo trip when he went MIA I thought better of that idea and agreed. It didn't make sense to drive two cars so we drove up in his. This time it was packed much more efficiently, I might add. Once we arrived there, the only glitch was where he was going to stay after Christmas and before he started his semester.

When he told me that Colleen's parents had offered to let him stay with them at their home I was amazed and relieved. All I can say is that there is a special place in heaven for them. They were so gracious and generous to a young man they had never even met. I am sure Colleen told them whatever past history she had to offer up, and yet they still were eager to offer their home to him. To this day I am grateful to them for that.

Upon our arrival I finally met Colleen and found her to be a loving and talented young woman. I liked her instantly. She was acceptant of Dana's past and they seemed to have a common ground of love and understanding. We spent a long time chatting and I felt that she was a young woman who could, hopefully, handle a relationship with Dana. Was I judging? You bet. At this point in Dana's life I was judging everything that affected him. I left him with her and her family after the holidays, cautiously optimistic.

The semester was about to begin and I wrote what I hoped would be the last bloody check for tuition I would ever have to write. By mid-January Dana moved out of Colleen's parent's home and into his dorm room, which by his standards was fairly bare boned but acceptable. He wasn't there to do anything but study. He had stayed with me almost six months and was seven months clean. Yes, we were all counting. That's what addicts and families of addicts do. They count, a lot. He then landed a job, always helpful when one has no money, working part-time for a pharmaceutical company as a Pharma Compliance Specialist. I surmised his experience with drugs was finally paying off. His job was to serve as a third-party liaison to review and audit applications to Pfizer's Patient Assistance program. This job he could do in in his room. Perfect.

With him gone I had time to reflect on all that had transpired. We had gotten through another tough time. He had survived and recovered. For that I was thankful. We then received news of another young man, also a former high school classmate of Dana's, who had not been so lucky and had died of an overdose. I could too easily imagine the pain and suffering that family was experiencing. Remembering the day Shanna and I searched for my son, hoping and fearing he wasn't dead, I felt so grateful that he was alive and doing well.

The financial cost for that wellness was not inconsequential. Ask the parent of any addict out there. I realized then, that year alone, I had spent $10,000 in tuition, $11,000 in rehab, and then the cost of his car. He had to stay clean. I couldn't do this any longer. Was it worth it? Absolutely. I couldn't bear the thought of the alternative. I was hoping and praying that he was strong enough to make it through his last semester. Did I even dare hope he would graduate in May? Remembering the disastrous weekend when he failed walk with his graduating class, I was trying to remain optimistic.

Throughout the semester I was on pins and needles. I was monitoring his progress from afar. It was difficult to not hear daily how he was faring. I longed to see him so I could assess the situation, but that was out of the question. He had to be given some space and I was going to have to trust that he could make his own decisions. Having already experienced two major "wake up" calls, though, I couldn't relax. I don't think the parent of any addict is ever fully relaxed. It's like there is this persistent cloud over our heads waiting to explode. For the past fifteen years, every time his name had appeared on my cell phone I experienced a mild panic attack, just knowing something was wrong. I felt like a Pavlovian dog reacting with a conditioned response.

By the end of February, Dana and Colleen had decided to move in together. Given his past few failed attempts to establish a live-in relationship with a woman, I wasn't particularly enthusiastic about this idea. But Colleen had found an apartment in Summit and together it was going to be affordable for them both. After listening to the pros of renting said apartment, I told him if that's what he really wanted to do then go ahead and good luck. My son was thirty-six years old at this time. He really didn't need Mom's approval. I was all too aware that many of his old friends from town were already quite successful in their careers. They had established lucrative jobs and some had already done well enough to purchase million-dollar homes. These same friends, however, were still supportive of Dana and continued to be there for him. If they judged, they kept it from him. It had to weigh on his mind, though, that his life was a far cry from what he had hoped for. At least having his own apartment could hopefully help him gain a little self-respect. This was not an argument he made regarding the renting of the apartment, but as a mom I knew he needed this.

It turned out to be a good move, which was certainly a novelty in "Dana's World." He was able to continue his at-home job while attending school. Colleen went about her business as a graphic artist at a nearby store. They cooked meals together and were able to spend some time at the Jersey Shore. Things were going better for Dana. He was on a course to normalcy.

I was counting the days until we found out if he was actually going to pass his course and graduate. I needed to know the score on every quiz, every test, and every exam. I literally had a lot invested in this. Many phone calls were made that last semester. How did you do? How do you think you did? What does that mean? Are you going to graduate? If I was going to fly up for a graduation I had to know in order to book a ticket. Did I dare purchase one in March? Should I wait until April? If he graduated, Shanna wanted to fly up too. She was going to also have to purchase a ticket and take time off work. We just needed to wait and hope. By mid-April he told us, yes, it looked like he was going to graduate. Hallelujah! It looked like life was finally going to change. How I so wanted that cloud removed. But more than anything, I wanted Dana to finally become a nurse.

Tickets purchased, bags packed, and practically jumping with happiness, I boarded the plane for New Jersey. Because of work, Shanna wasn't coming until the following day. On the flight up I recalled Dana's last highly anticipated graduation day from college, which turned into a nightmare for him and the entire family. Surely, that was not going to happen again. Maybe that's why his dad wasn't planning on attending this one. I was sure he had a good reason, but for whatever, he was not attending.

Dana picked me up at the airport and drove to his and Colleen's apartment. Located on the first floor of a large home with a huge wraparound porch, it was old but well maintained. I was pleased to see they had fixed it up with loving care and creativity. He had clearly been exercising his building skills again but this time his results were surprisingly recognizable and useful. It was uplifting to realize when sober, Dana had many creative talents. After giving me a tour, we all walked the quick two blocks into town for some lunch and much needed catch-up talks. That evening we went out to dinner, just Colleen, Dana, Joe, and I. Joe was still in the mix, but I had moved away some five years ago and our relationship was casual if not strained at this point. I had spent the past five years worrying about Dana and trying to create a life for myself in South Carolina. Hopefully the worrying aspect would change with the events of the following day.

There were only six tickets available for graduation. Shanna, Colleen, and I would account for three and Dana invited three buddies who had stood by him through everything and wanted to cheer for him during this momentous event. To begin the celebrated day and try and relax, Shanna and I treated ourselves to a mani-pedi at our favorite salon. We felt like we deserved it. (A week at a spa was what I really needed but had learned to settle for whatever was realistic.) By 5 p.m. we were more than ready to let the activities commence. Dana got dressed in his all-white outfit which he thought looked ridiculous. I liked it. I dressed in what I hoped was going to be a graduation dress I could wear again without evoking unpleasant memories. We piled into two cars and headed down to his campus where the pinning ceremony was to take place. Was this really going to happen?

Just thinking about that evening makes me teary. We arrived and found seats near an aisle so we could see him. As I looked around the auditorium and saw other families united to cheer on their loved one who was graduating, I wondered if they too felt the immense relief that I felt. The event was to be a life changer for so many. For the majority of the graduates, this was their first after high school. I knew Dana was older than most. Most of the nursing candidates were women, but we thought it was pretty cool that he was going to be a male nurse. Finally, all the candidates lined up and walked in. The six of us were just yelling at each other, "There he is, there he is!" He was indeed in line.

Several speeches were given as well as several awards. Dana didn't receive any special awards, which was fine by me. I just wanted to see him walk across the stage when his name was called. The moment finally arrived, and they called his name. He was graduating! It was

June 8, 2018. It had been fourteen years since the major disappointing, non-graduation from his college. So much had happened in that time, but he had persisted. I thought my heart would burst. I was so proud of what he had accomplished. I was one happy mommy. I couldn't help but wonder if there were any other recovering addicts on stage.

CHAPTER 19

A JOB!

GRADUATING FROM NURSING school doesn't automatically qualify one to become a nurse. First you must pass the state board exam. This was yet another hurdle that had to be crossed, so, fingers crossed, we all awaited the outcome of Dana's results. On July 11 he told all of us he had passed. His announcement came on Facebook: "Passed my state boards and officially a licensed RN! Only wish I could pick up the phone to tell Granddad . . . he would have been so proud." He posted a picture of himself, age six with his granddad.

He had hundreds of responses, but my favorite was from Julina who wrote, "Congrats, Dana, so well deserved! That picture brought tears to my eyes. Yes, he would have been so proud. You two had a special bond." Yes, we were all proud of him.

He now was able to experience some control over his life, and the bouts of depression and anxiety now seemed a thing of the past. Looking toward the future was having a positive effect as his job search began in full swing. After receiving several offers, he decided to accept a position at a jail in Somerset County. He started on August 23. His job was to provide care and assessment of the inmates, who varied in population from 220-400. While he was working there he received another offer from a large, well-known hospital. He liked his job at the jail but it was a long commute and after six months accepted the offer at the hospital. Having worked in a hospital before, he was familiar with and liked the constant activity. I wasn't enthusiastic about the location, but he told me the hospital was one of the best in the state.

He began his new job at the hospital in December 2018, working in geriatrics. I was thrilled that this time he really was on a positive career path. His life would be so different from what he had experienced over the past fourteen years. When people asked me then how Dana was doing, it gave me the utmost pleasure to finally say, "He's doing great!" He had a good job, a wonderful girlfriend, and a place to live.

For the first time in many years I found myself able to relax a bit. I opened my mind to meeting new people and was fortunate enough to meet a wonderful man, Mike, with whom I discovered I had much in common. Our love of golf brought us together. Many of my friends will take the credit for our having met, but in truth we found each other. I started enjoying my life for the first time in what felt like ages. We took trips together to play courses outside the state. We hiked, visited the amazing waterfalls in northern Georgia, and dined in out-of-the-way places. But mostly we played golf. My mind felt freer than in had in over a decade. The cloud had finally been lifted. I laughed and smiled more than I had in ages.

I was looking forward to the family all visiting in October. Dana was to come down and it would be his first trip to the island since he had completed his successful rehab with me. Julina's family was planning to also visit at that time and he wanted to be part of the family gathering. The week did not disappoint. The weather was fabulous, and we enjoyed beach picnics, bike rides, and golf games. Dana entertained us with stories about his job, the patients he had been assigned to care for, and the overall workings of the hospital. My favorite memory though was the day we all boarded a boat and headed out to one of the sandbars off-island.

It was a beautiful cloudless day. October has always been my favorite month in Hilton Head. The tourists were gone, the humidity was down, and the skies were sunny and blue. We had packed lunch for the eleven of us. After arriving at the sandbar, Dana jumped off the boat with all four of his nieces and proceeded to romp in the sand with them, throwing himself headlong onto the beach and letting them cover his entire body in sand. The screaming, laughing, and giggling was music to my ears. Seeing him so enjoy "his four little ladies" was heart lifting. He could only stay a few days because of his work, but the memory of that visit was special. To the girls, he was just Uncle Dana. He was not a recovering addict. They did not know what he had been through. Their love and acceptance of him was refreshing. It felt wonderful to finally have a normal family get-together.

Hoping to continue the momentum, I decided to fly up to Vermont with Shanna and her family for Thanksgiving at Julina's home. I was hoping Dana would be able to get time off to join us, but that was out of the question because of his work schedule. We awoke the following morning to more than a foot of snow, unheard of in Vermont for that time of year. We made the most of it and constructed massive snowmen, went sledding, and the younger ones went skiing. Dana so wanted to attend but spent that Thanksgiving with Colleen's family in New Jersey. We all missed him, especially the girls. We called him and sent pictures of our amazing snowmen. He told them he would try and make it up for Christmas.

It seemed the hospital needed people on staff that Christmas, so he didn't make it up to see his sister's family for the holidays. I didn't fly up either, having just visited during Thanksgiving. Instead, my new beau Mike and I went to Florida to visit friends and play golf. I felt after years of being "on watch" I was entitled to some R and R. Dana was doing well and enjoying his new status as an RN. All was good with the world. I was no longer checking in constantly with Dana. I knew he had it under control.

After the holidays I threw myself headlong into golf team play,

tennis team play, and arranging dates of visitation for my friends who
were planning trips down in the spring. Marybeth, my best friend from
high school, was coming down for her yearly trip. I so looked forward
to the fun times we were going to have. The last time she visited we
tried to sync my cell phone to my car. After several ridiculous, futile
attempts and collapsing with laughter, we decided to video our next
attempt. It wasn't meant to be funny, but somehow we got the giggles
and had to do four or five restarts. The end result finally paid off. We
finally achieved the sync. My God, were we clever or what? We played
our video back and lost it, laughing until we cried.

Thinking it might just be humorous to us, I showed it to my
daughter. She reluctantly agreed to watch it, thinking we were
exaggerating the hilarity of it. She and her husband nearly fell to the
floor laughing. Marybeth then decided to share it with one of our
high school friends, which turned out to be a big mistake. Rosie was
in charge of our fiftieth class reunion to take place that fall. At the
end of the reunion evening, there was a big surprise for everyone,
including us. There we appeared on the big screen, showing off
our abilities as senior "tech savvies." The room erupted in laughter.
We were somewhat embarrassed but still joined in the hysterical
laughter. It was just the two of us having fun and acting like teenagers
again. This type of diversion was what I was eagerly anticipating
when she next came down. Double trouble and lots of fun.

Marybeth arrived on the first Monday in May. I picked her up
at the Savannah airport and we caught up with each other's lives on
the ride to the island. Her first question was, "How is Dana doing?"

"Just great!" I answered enthusiastically. "He's working at Beth
Israel Hospital and loves it. He tells me his hours are good, the pay
is great, and finally in his life, he has benefits. This of course is great
for me as well because I haven't had to subsidize his life for the past
ten months."

I went on to describe his living arrangements with his girlfriend
Colleen and what a great supporter she had been to him. Marybeth

told me she was so glad for both of us. She could see I was practically hugging myself with happiness.

The topic then shifted to what we were planning to do while she was visiting. I told her we had booked a tee time for the following day over at the Marine Base on Parris Island. I explained to her that it had an awesome public course, very reasonably priced and with unsurpassed low country wildlife. (This means lots of big gators.) I then told her about my favorite sign on the course, posted for those unwitting people who don't seem to understand wildlife: "Common Sense and South Carolina law dictate that you do not feed the alligators!" She looked a little unsettled. I assured her they would leave us alone if we left them alone. That evening we went to our favorite haunt, celebrated, took pictures of one another, and gleefully posted them for our high school friends to see how we had restarted our week of antics.

The next morning we were looking forward to a great day as Mike accompanied us on our golf outing. We headed out early to the Marine base, hoping to grab some breakfast at their amazing snack bar adjacent to the pro shop. We arrived and unloaded our clubs. As we were approaching the snack bar, though, I saw I had a missed call from Dana. He hadn't left a message, which I thought was odd. I told that to Marybeth. She said he probably had some good news, like he got a promotion, and wanted to tell me in person. I didn't think so. I tried to call him back but he didn't answer, so I left him a message.

We grabbed our breakfast sandwiches, but as we headed toward the practice range I received another call. This one was from Dylan, my ex-husband. Suddenly feeling very apprehensive, I answered it. *This could not be good news*, I thought. Why after months was he calling me now? When I answered he said, "Linda, this is Dylan. Have you talked to Dana?"

I told him no, I hadn't. He had called and I had missed it and he hadn't returned my call.

"I don't know how to tell you this," Dylan said, "but he has been fired from his job. They caught him with drugs."

I felt like someone had just punched me in the gut. I went numb. And then I just sat down and cried. Ask the parent of any addict. You don't know when the next shoe is going to drop. Life can be a living hell.

CHAPTER 20

AGAIN

DANA FINALLY CALLED me several hours later. He was crying, and I was unglued. What had happened? He confessed that he had been taking some pills for pain relief. He still was experiencing pain from previous problems and had ready access to the drugs. He knew he shouldn't have, but he did. Someone saw him and reported it, and the hospital had no option but to fire him. Was he going to lose his license? He wasn't sure.

My anger and frustration at that moment was unprecedented. All I could think about was that he had wasted four years of college. Four years of nursing school. For what? It was all a total waste of money. It was a waste of *my* money. Now he certainly had no job opportunities. I couldn't believe he hadn't been arrested and thrown in jail. And what was going to happen with Colleen? Surely she would be as fed up as I was and throw his ass out, as others had in the past. And then there was his family, his siblings, and their husbands. There went any respect from them he had managed to regain over the past few years. As I internalized these thoughts, I realized he was trying to explain something. I finally listened.

He was trying to tell me about RAMP. I had no idea what this was. I was still reeling from the blow of his terrible news, but I forced myself to listen. He was trying to explain that this problem of his was not uncommon among nurses. It was so common, in fact, that an entire program had been developed and enacted to help those who had fallen victim to being around the prevalence of so many drugs. The program was called RAMP, which is an acronym for Recovery and Monitoring Program.

This program was established in 2003 in New Jersey as an Alternative to Discipline program. Managed by the Institute for Nursing for the New Jersey Board of Nursing, it is designed to encourage health professionals to seek a recovery program before their impairment harms a patient or damages their careers through a disciplinary action. The New Jersey State Board of Nursing refers nurses who qualify to RAMP for monitoring as an alternative to disciplinary action. RAMP participation is also part of the reinstatement process for nurses with a licensing action.

After he had told me a bit about the program and that he had already called someone from RAMP, I felt the slightest glimmer of hope. Maybe all was not lost. He seemed relieved to know this program existed and that they would accept him into it. That was at least some good news. But the reality stood. He would not be working any time soon.

I dove into researching the program. I was not surprised to read that in 2016 over twenty-seven million people in the United States reported current use of illicit drugs or misuse of prescription drugs. Apparently, health professionals are not immune to this disease. The American Nurses Association estimated that 7-8 percent of nurses were using drugs or alcohol to an extent that was sufficient to impair professional performance. My son fell right into that 7-8 percent. Feeling frustrated and disappointed about this, but grateful that professionals had acknowledged these facts and set up a program, I stepped back to see what came next.

Logistics had to be dealt with. The program only operated in New Jersey, so he would have to stay there. Dana had already had his intake interview. No shock that he qualified for the program. That was step one. Step two: He had to show up for a meeting the following day. Colleen had to work, but he could not drive his car. Apparently, he was still high on whatever he was taking. Someone had to take him, but I was not there. It was imperative he show up, and on time. Now what?

As I had done so many times in the past, I phoned a friend. This time it was Diane. There is a place in heaven for her, as well. When I telephoned her she immediately stepped up and agreed to help. She picked him up the next day at his apartment and drove him to his meeting. I was so afraid he was going to miss the meeting by oversleeping, but he was up and ready when she arrived. She kept me posted all day, patiently waiting for him until the meeting was over and then taking him to lunch. I love her. She did what I couldn't do because I wasn't there.

While I was awaiting the outcome of this meeting, I decided to write a somewhat scathing email. I suppose I did this out of total frustration at what I had learned. This one was sent to the new psychiatrist Dana had found, who had written a prescription for him for Adderall. When I learned this I became enraged.

"How is it," I wrote, "that there seems to be a national database for nearly everything in our lives and you doctors do not have a database for people with a known addiction? I think it's imperative that this problem be addressed."

I told him that he had prescribed a drug to a recovering addict. In fact, it was the same drug that I believed caused Dana's addiction in the first place. He replied, expressing his sorrow that it had happened. That's it. Shame on you.

So, Dana prepared to enter yet another program. This time he went to a facility in south Jersey. I was relieved that Colleen agreed to take him down, not just because of the transportation issue, but because she apparently had decided to hang in there and not abandon Dana when he needed help. Her status in my estimation grew leaps and bounds. And so it was, on May 9, that Dana entered his third rehab facility. They say the third time's a charm. *Let's see about that,* I thought.

The staff on site was going to assess him and after five days give a decision. We were all hoping that he would then be allowed to begin an outpatient program. Collectively they decided that this was the best option for him. He assured me he knew what he had to do and what was expected of him, but we had all heard that before. This time, however, he was to be monitored every day. He had to attend a meeting every day. He had to have a blood test every week. I was encouraged. If I wasn't there to monitor, then someone else had to. There was no way he was going to be allowed to reenter nursing if he slipped up this time. His life--and career—now depended upon it.

Shortly after starting his third rehab program, Dana phoned me. He had just gotten word that his friend Chris, from YANA, had died. The obvious question was, from what? Unfortunately, the obvious answer was from a drug overdose. He was Dana's age and had a wife. He wouldn't live to see the birth of their baby boy who was due in November. It was too familiar, all too heartbreaking and too much of a reminder of what the next phone call might be. Things were certainly not perfect, but at least Dana was still with us. And we all were doing everything we could to have it remain that way.

When he entered the program, he wasn't allowed to work. All focus was to be on the rehab process. He was not even allowed to serve as an EMT. Their strict rules thankfully allowed no access to any type of drugs. The question remained as to what he was now going to do with his time. I hoped that he would spend a lot of it reflecting upon his past choices.

He and Colleen decided to get a dog. My daughters thought it a rather ridiculous idea, as it seemed Dana was hardly able to care for himself, let alone introduce another factor into the equation. Dogs can also be a tremendous expense, they argued. They should know since they have dogs themselves, some the size of small ponies. Despite this, I thought it a good idea. Dana was home alone for the most part and at least it would give him companionship and a good reason to go for long walks. He needed the exercise. As it turned out, the decision was in fact a game-changer in my estimation. For the first time in a long time Dana seemed genuinely happy and had a focus on something else other than himself.

It seemed everything was under control for the time being. I was turning 70 and started thinking about taking a trip with Mike for an early celebration. Did I dare go away? Should we leave the country? Was I being too optimistic this time? We discussed it at length and finally opted on a ten-day river cruise in Europe starting in Prague and ending in Paris. Excitedly, we planned and planned. Two other friends were to go with us. Just in case, I made sure my cell phone could receive calls. One never knew what might come up. I had already had too many surprise phone calls from Dana over the years to feel totally comfortable in leaving the country. I could just envision seeing his name come up on my cell phone as I was finally walking through the Musee d'Orsay in Paris or strolling along the Seine.

Please! I thought. *Don't ruin this special moment for me. Please just be safe and don't do anything stupid.* Fingers crossed, we packed and set out.

The trip was an unbelievable success and, to my great relief and surprise, no bad news arrived while we were away. Our only moment of frustration came when we finally returned to the States only to encounter a taxi driver in New Jersey who spoke not a word of English. He spoke Arabic and Spanish. I opted for the Spanish and we arrived at our hotel, less than one mile away. He also tried overcharging us. Forty dollars, seriously? We weren't having it. Our treatment by Parisians far surpassed that of people from New Jersey. However, I was deeply grateful for the program Dana was in, actually unique to New Jersey, so I guess I should cut the state some slack. It was great having someone else to watch over my son. I loved those people monitoring him.

My daughters then decided to hold a family gathering in Vermont that August, partially in celebration of my birthday. I was really hoping that Dana and Colleen could join us. The strict program, however, had to be adhered to. He could not miss his daily meetings or his blood checks. We were all disappointed but knew that the bigger and more important issue was for him to do what was required of him. It was hard to explain to his nieces why he wasn't there. They have been kept in the dark about his addiction. They are young but now getting older. They will find out one day soon enough.

Because of the program he had not been allowed to travel or visit with the family for months. I imagine this is one of the most difficult parts of recovery. If we lived closer it wouldn't have been an issue at all but, unfortunately, it wasn't the biggest issue. He called me the beginning of October to say he had just been to the dentist after experiencing severe pain. As a result of extended drug use, his teeth had decayed to the point that he had to have five teeth extracted.

My mind weighed the extended damage that collectively had taken a toll on him. His body was not in great shape. He continued to have pain due to the epididymitis. For this he had to see a specialist for pain management as he couldn't take the usual prescribed pain medications. His teeth were a horror. He had already had several removed, several root canals, and now this current costly diagnosis. He had been to the ER countless times. He had endured two operations, and that didn't include his kidney donation. Not only was he physically in poor shape, but over the past sixteen years his debt had accumulated in spite of the fact that I had subsidized him for so long. His medical expenses alone were upwards of $100,000. His financial status was abysmal. He had been to three rehab facilities. He had suffered the loss of several jobs and lost his nursing license.

I believe that all of this occurred because of that first prescription of Adderall, a study drug. I have read story after story of similar nightmares. Because of our own nightmare I have come to believe that it can ruin a young person's life as well as well as those around him as well. I wish he had never been prescribed the drug. I am not convinced he ever needed it in the first place. As I am sure so many do, I get so angry just thinking about it. But dwelling on the past doesn't solve the problem going forward. I continued to remain determined that history would not repeat itself and Dana could somehow move forward with a productive life.

By October things were looking hopeful. Dana had completed most of his program and was allowed to leave the area for a bit. He came down to Hilton Head for a visit and we talked a lot about his future. The RAMP program included assistance in job placement once all the requirements had been met. He could not work in a hospital. That was obvious, as the program didn't allow any access to drugs. The news was a relief and a blessing. The staff obviously knew the potential ramifications of placing anyone with a history of abuse in a facility administering drugs. Dana didn't have a clue where he would end up but was very eager to get back to work. He was getting bored, in spite of the dog. He was taking lots of walks, attending meetings, and cleaning his apartment. He still had three more months to complete the program, so his life was on hold for the time being.

In December Dana and Colleen decided to go north and visit Julina and her family. Shockingly, his dad decided to drive up and spend Christmas with all of them as well. He wasn't around for much of this journey, except for emails and the rare phone call. This wasn't completely his fault since Dylan was dealing with poor health at this point. I was just glad they all got to spend Christmas together. It was a time that hopefully Dana could start anew to regain the trust of his sister and brother-in-law and renew some family ties.

For a time, Julina and her husband did not even want Dana around their girls. While that may seem harsh, in reality it was probably a good idea. Unfortunately, in addition to losing their health, their teeth, their money, and their jobs, addicts lose this other most important aspect of their lives, the respect and trust of their families. The love was always there, but the trust was something that had to be regained over time. It seemed like a good time to work on this. Unfortunately, Dana became extremely ill that week with some sort of bug and wasn't able to spend as much time with the family as he had hoped. That part was a shame as it was the first time in over twenty years that his dad had been with even part of the family for the holidays.

Once the holidays had passed, Dana turned his attention to trying to secure a job. First his nursing license had to be reinstated. We waited for that news with bated breath until it happened. Then, with the help of the people at his RAMP program, his hope of landing a new job became a reality. He started his new position in March at a nearby dialysis center.

He had been practically sequestered at home for the past nine months, completing his program and getting his act together. It was pretty ironic that, only days after starting in his new position, the State of New Jersey issued a stay-at-home mandate for the entire state because of COVID-19. Because he was a nurse, however, he was needed so he did indeed go to his job. He was up at 4 a.m. for an early arrival at 5 a.m. For the first time in the history of man, the Garden State Parkway (AKA parking lot) was devoid of vehicles. He kept telling me how eerie it was. People on the road were being stopped and asked their place of destination. Only necessary personnel were allowed on the roads. Nurses all across the nation became indispensable and became heroes within a matter of days.

CHAPTER 21

THE ENDING

AS I WRITE these words, it is July 2020. Dana still has his job, his girlfriend, and his dog. He has created his own family. For the most part he has his life back. I hope and pray every day that it remains that way. I have come to learn that I have no control over the outcome. This is all up to Dana. The family and I can give him love and support, but ultimately he has to be the one who determines the outcome of his life.

When he finally read this story, Dana wanted to make one thing perfectly clear. In no way does he regret the decision he made to donate his kidney. He feels this is one good decision he has made in his life, to save another's. Regardless of the outcome of his past relationship with Karen's daughter, he still feels it was the right thing to do. His other comment was to my surprise, that the story was incredibly accurate.

In telling this story I realized I have been very hard on myself. So many times I felt like I could have or should have been able to fix the problem, because as I mentioned before, that's what moms want to do. I also came to realize that I did remain stubborn in my efforts. I was determined to do the best I could on my own. It is now apparent to me that as a single mom I was so caught up in my work that I probably ignored or was oblivious to the early signs of his addiction. I only know that I did the best that I could. My efforts always had his wellbeing in my mind. I would want to be remembered for that—as a mom who would go to extremes to save her son and not give up.

Unfortunately for Dana, there was not a father nearby or even a father figure to get in his face when his problems all first started. Perhaps if one had been present Dana may not have fallen into the all-consuming trap that would rob him of many years. This for so many reasons did not and could not happen. I realize now that our family was, in fact, not so normal after all. Girls, you were right. In telling this story I have learned we were perhaps more dysfunctional than I had thought. While I tried to be the glue to hold everyone together, there were factors out of my control which affected me personally and in turn affected all of my children. While this did not cause Dana's problem, it didn't help his situation one bit.

When it was first revealed to me that my son was an addict, I was quick to blame others. It couldn't have been his fault, I thought. Though Dana did in fact make bad choices during all those years, I am still not convinced that this nightmare could have been avoided had he not been so quickly prescribed a drug to help him study. This highly addictive drug is a danger to so many when it is not monitored correctly. Addicts quickly learn that when they cannot get the dosage or quantities they crave by legal means, they can go doctor shopping. When one doctor has no clue what the other has prescribed, that makes a recipe for disaster. One can only hope that the medical community will recognize the absurdity of this system and do something about it. A database truly needs to be created. A patient may be turned away at a pharmacy but can easily turn to another.

In sharing this story with the twists and turns that both Dana and I experienced, it has become apparent to me that he made choices that did not involve me. I was always there to pick up the pieces, and I do not regret having done that. While many parents have told me they would have thrown his ass out after the first round, I could never imagine doing that. I experienced pain, disappointment, anger, and frustration for those sixteen years—years I would love to have back. I have spent all of that time waiting for the next shoe to drop, but that is what life dealt me. Most importantly, I still have Dana, unlike so many unfortunate families who have lost their loved ones to this insidious disease of drug abuse.

The only thing I have truly lost is money, lots of money. While I have had pages and pages of expenses in front of me during this whole time, I never added them up until now. I think I have been afraid to know. I guessed randomly that I had spent about $100,000 on Dana since his addiction took hold, and my guess wasn't far off the mark. When I tallied the expenses, the total was $99,630. More than $30,000 of that was for medical expenses that are far from paid off, if I'm not mistaken. I am wide awake now and know that my girls will be horrified.

Girls, if you are reading this, I am so sorry. I hope more than anything in my life you will never have to experience anything like this. Knowing the way you love your girls, I am sure you would do the same for them, but God forbid that should ever happen. I thought, too, that I had a normal life at your age. I only hope that you will be more awake than I was. Maybe this will help you. Or maybe it might help someone else.

I know that I have only really touched the tip of the iceberg with this memoir. This story is my perception of what Dana went through. From his perspective I know there is so, so much more. I didn't experience the pain he felt, the depression he experienced, or the spiraling loss of control. I didn't experience the depths he went to obtain the drugs when he was using. I only know that there were methods that no parent would be proud of. But I understand that's what happens. Hopefully, it will happen no more. The experience for me was costly and emotional. But more than the money, I wanted Dana to have his life. Fortunately, he does.

Everything I have been through has been worth it to me. Dana has lost so much more than I have, and he is all too aware of it. This was not the life I wanted for my only son. Ironically, as I finish my story today, it is his birthday. Thirty-eight years ago when I held that small baby in my arms, I did not envision this life for him. But he is picking up the pieces and moving ahead each day. He is finally able to realize his dream of nursing, a career that hopefully will take him far in his life.

It is months later now as I finish the final editing of my story. Dana started a new job this week as an intake nurse at a rehab center. A fitting end to his story. Dana, I can only hope and pray that you stay healthy, stay happy and stay clean. You can repay me by doing all of this and living your life to the fullest.

When he read my story—his story—he expressed to me that I missed so much. Yes, I did. That is the point. I missed things I should have seen. He wanted people to know the real truth about some of the events that took place. So I asked him some questions—some of my unanswered questions which reveal the true destructive path his life took. His written responses are candid and shed yet another perspective on the effects of abuse.

In college, when did you start amping up your dosage of your meds?

I started increasing my dosage right away. From the very first time I was prescribed I started taking more than the written dosage. I never started doctor shopping while I was in college but from the very beginning I started to manipulate the system however I could to get more. I would tell my doctor that I had lost meds or that the prescription was stolen or whatever I could think of to get more. He was a very old man and I think he was naïve in what was going on and believed quite a bit of what I was saying. It was also known however who amongst our group of friends had prescriptions because these meds were often shared with other people to help with studying. We called them our study buddies. For that reason I was also able to get more meds from other people because they were given/sold/ traded so freely among students.

How many doctors were prescribing to you in college? Did you think you had a problem then?

When I was in college I don't think I ever had more than one doctor but I was able to get more meds in other ways (explained above). The thing about addiction is that the tolerance and craving develops gradually over time. If I had been self-medicating with the dosages I was taking at the very end during the early months and years of my addiction I probably would've died. The tolerance develops gradually over time,. just like with drinking.

When you went abroad to Budapest were you able to buy drugs there?

The answer to this question is yes, but the drugs that we bought there were ecstasy and marijuana and all of us were using these (mostly ecstasy) to party with. Prior to arriving in Budapest when we were staying in Romania, I got real drunk one night by myself (this was the Hotel Topaz thing) and I completely blacked out and slept through my midterm the next day. That day was really rough for me and I remember even to this day, very clearly, telling my friend that I might have a prescription drug problem. He knew that I was prescribed Adderall and he asked me to hand over my meds to him. You may not remember but I told you that either I had lost my prescription or that I lost it but nonetheless I had you fill a prescription for me and asked you to bring it when you visited. Obviously, I never told him that I asked you to bring me another prescription, but when you visited me in Budapest you did bring me more. I remember that I was actually experiencing withdrawal symptoms, which mainly consisted of not being able to stay awake and the constant thought of getting more. To this day I remember the relief I felt when you arrived.

When you were working in the city at AIG did you recognize at the time it was probably going to jeopardize your job or did you feel you had everything under control?

I think at that point if I had really known about addiction what I know now, I might have had even a small glimpse of some sort of rational thought or perspective on this matter. At that point however (with the exception of what happened at my graduation and a few of my experiences living abroad) I hadn't ever suffered the consequences of my disease. I do remember the morning that I slept through my alarm and my boss called the house, and I think that's when I realized that something was wrong with me but I never considered stopping because I knew the effect that would have had on my mind and my body. The only answer to the problem at that point was getting more.

Why did you go to the hospital in Myrtle Beach?

I remember I went to an urgent care center because I was having pain and I'm pretty sure that I knew it was epididymitis. I don't know if I went with the specific intent of getting relief from narcotics or what, but I do know that they found something that warranted transferring me to the hospital. I'm not sure what they gave me in the ambulance but I remember I liked it and the rest of that entire experience it's very foggy. The only thing I remember to this day about that ordeal (with the exception of being at the urgent care facility since I remember speaking to granddad on the phone) is being in the ICU and even that is a blur.

Describe what happened when Granddad died.

Honestly I'm not quite sure what happened when Granddad died. What I remember is the fact that I had very little emotional response. His death definitely came as a shock to me because I had not been given any information about how far along the disease had already progressed. What I do remember is the fact that my emotional response did not seem proportional to the response I thought I should have had. Because I knew so little about addiction I didn't know that drugs were used to completely numb yourself from the outside world. I definitely know that my drug usage increased following Granddad's death and I devoted all of my time and focus on making a slideshow for his funeral. The slideshow was actually really helpful in helping me to cope with granddad's death because it allowed me to look back on his life and reflect at all the moments he spent with me and the rest of his family and it allowed me to eventually look at his face without seeing pain. I guess looking at his pictures and watching the videos, it was put in front of me very clearly this reality that he was gone.

How many doctors were prescribing to you in Myrtle Beach?

I'm pretty sure that the most number of doctors that were prescribing me at one time when I was living there was three. I remember that one of the doctors was actually located in North Carolina and was about an hour drive away. There were a limited number of psychiatrists in the Myrtle Beach and surrounding areas and for some reason that was the closest one I could find that I was not already using. Also I was forced to find a new doctor after I was caught forging (doctoring) one of my other doctor's prescriptions.

Please describe what you told me about altering prescriptions.

The first time I ever altered a prescription was when a doctor had written me a prescription for 30 mg of Adderall and I knew that the maximum daily dosage was 60 mg. What I would do is sit down at a desk with a bright light and very precisely and carefully use a razor blade to ever so delicately scratch at the ink so as not to cut through the paper but remove the top layer of ink. There was a learning curve for being able to do this and there were several times I ruined the prescription. Consequently, I would go back to my doctor and ask him to write it again telling him I'd lost it. I quickly learned the hard way that most doctors were very reluctant to do this because they knew a lost prescription could be filled just as easily as the second one they were asked to write so they had to use blind faith in believing what you were telling them was true. What happened with one of the doctors in Myrtle Beach was that this plan backfired on me. By that time it wasn't enough to get just a maximum daily dosage.

I needed a whole new prescription. One of the times I came in for an office visit I was very high on uppers and I hadn't slept in a long time. For that reason I looked like complete shit and my eyes were totally bloodshot. He asked what was wrong with my eyes and I told him that my allergies were really bad and were only made worse by being out on the golf course. He then volunteered to write me a prescription for allergy medication and I knew right away I could use this to my advantage. It was easy to alter one number but trying to scrape off and write in an entirely new medication turned out to be more difficult than I realized. I got it right the first few times and got them filled but I can tell you going in to pick up the prescription was pretty terrifying. I always made sure to try and look my best and seem like an upstanding citizen. I really didn't want to drive attention to myself. I think it was the third time, however, in trying to alter the prescription I almost tore through the whole paper and the mistake was obvious. In hopes of covering up the mistake I decided to pour coffee on the prescription over the ruined area because I figured if the paper was stained the mistake wouldn't look so obvious. That time it worked. The next time--not so lucky. When I went to pick it up I was caught and was confronted by the pharmacist. I was lucky that they didn't report this to law enforcement; rather instead they reported it to my doctor. That just meant I needed a new doctor. I left the golf program and went home because I thought I was going to be arrested.

What crazy things happened in Myrtle Beach?

Strangely enough the craziest things that happened in Myrtle were related to things I did on my own. That's what "loners" do. They do things alone. Even though I lived with two roommates and was in a school with a whole bunch of guys who loved to party, I never got into the scene they were all involved in. I told myself that I was not like other kids who go to college and use drugs and get blackout drunk partying. I didn't have a drug or alcohol problem. I very rarely drank more than two or three beers and most nights I didn't drink at all. I convinced myself that I didn't have a problem with drugs because I was taking medications that were prescribed to me by a doctor. I was in denial about the fact multiple doctors were prescribing me and I wasn't taking the meds as prescribed.

My favorite thing to do in Myrtle Beach and what I remember most was going to the range at night at the Legends golf resort to practice. The range was open to the public and it was the only range you could go to at night. Practicing during the day was miserable simply because of how hot and humid it gets so it could only be done in small dosages. Being able to practice at night the temperature was much cooler and I could practice for much longer. The Legends golf resort was one of the nicest in the surrounding Myrtle Beach area and the range at night under the lights made everything feel very surreal. There is a long road through a lot of swampy area to get to the resort and it made you feel like you were in a very remote and private area. There was nothing but pristinely manicured grass, rolling fairways and tall reeds throughout. Simply by being there it was hard for me to think about anything but golf because the outside world suddenly didn't exist. This perception, although it was very real, was only magnified by my drug usage. A bottle of amphetamines combined with my physical surroundings made me feel like I was invincible on the course. It's impossible not to become hyper-focused in that state of mind. The way I practiced became very regimented and I approached each shot like I were on the course. When I first started doing this my hands would become blistered and a few times even started bleeding, but after a while my hands adapted and became nothing but callous. Unfortunately, muscle memory is very short-term when you are strung out so the end product of a good session on the range never once stuck with me.

The other thing I would do which is crazy was going out on the course I lived on at night to hawk golf balls. Golf balls are expensive, and I knew I could save a lot of money by going out and finding my own but the lengths that I would go to and doing this was a bit extreme. When my drug usage got really bad, I really only slept every other night. After getting a good night's rest and taking enough Adderall the next day I never wanted to go to sleep so I did a lot of strange things. One of the holes of the course I lived on replicated the 17th hole of TPC Sawgrass. It's a short hole to an island green so there was an endless supply of golf balls. This was a very nice resort course and green fees were high so the people playing this course almost always played with brand new pro V1s or balls comparable. Finding the balls at night, was visually easier because I would use a very bright flashlight and it would illuminate the golf balls at the bottom. I would always bring an old backpack because the balls I put in it smelled like crap from the lagoons. I would come home fill a bathtub with water add bleach and clean my balls in the bathtub all while my roommates were sleeping. A normal person might do all this, but I did this secretively at night. I never wanted people to know that I was pulling all-nighters hawking balls because I understood the insanity of it all and I didn't need to draw attention to myself. I was paranoid at that point and was always worried about what other people were thinking about me.

Did you ever wish for family intervention when you knew you had a problem?

I can say for certain that I never once wished for family intervention. My biggest fear in the world was being caught or found out. I distinctively remember one day I started to think about the importance Adderall had on my life. I asked myself whether I could quit if someone paid me a million dollars and without hesitation I knew (at least I thought I knew) that I could not do it.

Do you even remember either of your sisters' weddings?

I think I vaguely remember Shanna's wedding. There are bits and pieces I can remember of it. I remember being on the beach and watching the guy with the metal detector carry on about his business while the ceremony was going on. I remember how odd it all seemed. I remember being in the hotel room with all the groomsmen right before we walked out for the ceremony because that was the first time I learned (from one of the other groomsmen) how sick Mike's brother was and it affected me. I remember smoking cigars on the porch, I remember dancing in a Conga line, I remember etching my name on the plate we all signed. Considering how long ago it was I guess you could say I remember quite a bit. Julina's wedding I don't remember quite so much. I remember I brought Leticia as my date because we had just started dating and I was a bit love struck with her but it likely was due to the fact she was drop dead gorgeous and way out of my league lol. I actually remember being at a bar after the reception and at one point I think Dad even started hitting on her . . . which was very strange but I sort of got it. I remember piling into the back of someone's car to get to that bar afterwards. I'm not quite sure who was driving . . . whoever they were I know they were not sober. I remember bits and pieces of the rehearsal dinner. I generally remember the setting of where the ceremony took place but what I remember the most clearly was the argument I got into with Leticia at the hotel. I sort of knew at that point it was over and I guess I was paying more attention to her than I was on the event and the people we were there for.

When you were in nursing school (living with Bethany) and had been clean all those years, what precipitated your drug use?

What prompted that relapse was that in the back of my mind my clean date was sort of blurry because of the drugs I had been taking after my surgery and I knew what I did was not sober behavior. In speaking with one of the technicians we somehow started talking about Adderall and he told me that he took a different type of medication as an alternative to Adderall. This immediately got my attention as I thought perhaps my problem wasn't addiction but maybe it was Adderall. He told me about a medication called Provigil which is used to treat sleep shift work syndrome and narcolepsy. The basic difference between it and Adderall is that it's used to treat wakefulness rather than focus. I learned that it didn't make you quite as jumpy or give you quite the same high so I guess I convinced myself this was a great alternative. I looked at it as the middle ground between Straterra (non-narcotic ADHD medication) and Adderall. My doctor of course prescribed me Provigil because I convinced him to and only a month or two later I was back on Adderall.

After you finally became a nurse what caused you to start using again?

I remember the first time I took a narcotic from the hospital I was treating a young guy (in his twenties) who had surgery on his foot. I remember offering him a Percocet that I had already pulled from the drawer assuming he would take it because he had taken it earlier in the day and he told me he was in pain. When he told me he only wanted Tylenol I knew that meant I would have to waste the drug and for some reason I knew just how easy it would be for me to document that it was given and take it myself.

Lastly, and probably the hardest, can you talk about the one thing you most regret having done?

I'm not sure there's one moment or instance that I regret the most. Obviously stealing from you is at the very top of that list but what I think about the most often is what happened at AIG. It's not so much what I did there on one particular day to one particular person, it's the mystery about how different my life would look today if I wasn't an addict. It's knowing that I was in such the perfect position to have a lucrative career in finance and/or insurance and all the things that come with a large bank account. Also, add to that list, my graduation. Having to tell Grandma and Granddad the night before my graduation, right after Grandma gave me that blanket she had made as a congratulations gift. I guess I just regret not having done what I needed to do in submitting the right assignments to the right place at the right time before graduation to prevent the catastrophe that will never escape me. I still have dreams about scenarios surrounding the abrupt turn of events on the role my drug usage played in all of it.

He answered everything so candidly. I wasn't that surprised. He wanted his experiences known. After getting his responses to all my questions, I realize it only serves as a painful reminder of how the past sixteen years for Dana have been, for the most part, just a blurred memory. That part saddens me the most. These are years he'll never get back.

POSTSCRIPT

I HAVE RECENTLY learned that New Jersey has adopted a centralized database to track opioid prescriptions. As far as I can determine, it is used by physicians and pharmacies but not psychiatrists. Neither Adderall nor Lexapro are opioids, so this policy would not affect their use. Apparently, this new database only tracks patients for a year. The other fallacy is that hospital networks do not share with one another.

At least it is a start.

BIBLIOGRAPHY

"About Ramp." <www.https:/njsna.org> 14 Mar. 2020

Category Blog. "Longtime Hilltoppers Head Coach Keith Nixon
    Stepping Down After 28 Years

at Summit." 13 Aug. 2019 <www.summithockey.net> 15 Feb. 2020

Dahl, Melissa. "Watch a Brief Explainer on How Adderall Works."
    11 May

2015<www.thecut.com> 4 Feb. 2020

Diluna, Amy. "Man gives new life to girlfriend's mother-by donating
    his kidney." 1 Dec. 2015

<www.today.com> 10 Feb. 2020

Green Day. "Good Riddance." *Nimrod*, Reprise, 17 Oct. 1997

CPSIA information can be obtained
at www.ICGtesting.com
Printed in the USA
BVHW081156110821
614085BV00008B/523

9 781646 634118